MAKE SOME NEW PUDDINGS

270 RECIPES FOR WAR-TIME

CONTENTS

CONTENTS

CHAPTER III. BAKED PUDDINGS

CHAPTER IV. COLD PUDDINGS, BLANCMANGES, JELLIES, AND VARIOUS SWEET DISHES TO SERVE COLD

BLANCMANGES

JELLIES

CHAPTER V. PANCAKES, FRITTERS, SWEET OMELETS, AND CROQUETTES

PANCAKES

PLAINER PANCAKES

——— FRITTERS

SWEET OMELETS

CROQUETTES

CHAPTER VI. CREAMS, CUSTARDS, JUNKETS, AND TRIFLES

CHAPTER VII. FRUIT DISHES

CHAPTER VIII. PASTRY DISHES : FRUIT PIES, AMERICAN PIES, TARTS, AND OTHER PASTRIES

PASTRY MADE WITHOUT SHORTENING

CONTENTS

FRUIT PIES

AMERICAN PIES

TARTS

VARIOUS PASTRY

CHAPTER

GENERAL REMARKS

IF there be in all this world a dish peculiarly, notoriously, and one may say exclusively British, it is the Pudding. Other countries have other concoctions, with which they endeavour to replace this precious desideratum of England: sweet dishes rich and indigestible, light and ethereal, solid and fruity, or creamy and succulent; but they are not puddings. In no circumstances do we like the idea of doing without our puddings, and there is no reason why we should.

The recipes in this book have been selected for simplicity and economy, but they are all nourishing and delicious.

ECONOMY HINTS

Egg-powder can be used instead of eggs.

Custard-powder can be used instead of true custard ingredients.

Flour can be mixed with maize-flour or flaked maize.

Sugar can be reduced in quantity; or golden syrup, honey, or dried fruits can be substituted for it.

FLAVOURINGS

Flavourings are sometimes classed as luxuries; but this is unjustifiably austere. The flavour of a pudding, apart from the natural intrinsic flavour of its ingredients, is a very important thing, especially in the case of starchy compounds, such as puddings made of rice, cornflour, tapioca, macaroni, etc. These are otherwise apt to be exceedingly monotonous in the eating. But it is almost worse to overdo the flavouring, than to have none at all.

The best flavourings, perhaps, are the actual original articles—*i.e.* lemon peel instead of lemon extract, almonds instead of ratafia, vanilla bean instead of vanilla essence, saffron, nutmeg, cloves, ginger, cinnamon, freshly made coffee or tea. Next to these come the extracts and essences, and prepared articles, such as chocolate, caramel, orange-flower water, and rose-water. Liqueurs and cordials, especially curaçao, noyau, kirsch, and maraschino, impart a peculiarly delicate quality of flavour; sherry and rum are also employed, and claret is used for sauces. It is a mistake, however, to add any alcoholic flavouring to a hot dish; it is better added at the last moment (when the mixture is cooked) to dishes intended for serving cold. Whenever possible, wait till the dish is quite cold.

Remember that flavouring, of whatever kind, should be added *as late as possible* in the cooking, just before you remove a preparation from the fire. Otherwise it becomes evaporated, or dissipated, and loses half its value.

Of course this rule cannot apply to baked dishes : it is perhaps best to use fairly powerful flavourings for these, such as lemon, cinnamon, nutmeg, etc.

Combined Flavourings :—

> Lemon and vanilla
> Almond and vanilla
> Cinnamon and chocolate
> Chocolate and vanilla
> Caramel and almond
> Orange and almond

may be successfully combined.

Saffron imparts not only a characteristic and delicious taste, but a charming aroma and a rich colour to those dishes in which it is employed. It used to be immensely popular in England, but is now unduly neglected, except among Jewish families.

N.B.—Never leave out of anything whatsoever the necessary pinch of salt! It will make all the difference to the flavour; like good words in the proverb, it is "worth much, and costs little."

WEIGHTS AND MEASURES

2 saltspoons full . . .	= 1 coffeespoon.
2 coffeespoons . . .	= 1 teaspoon.
55 drops	= 1 teaspoon.
5 teaspoons (dry) . .	= 1 tablespoon.
4 teaspoons (liquid) . .	= 1 tablespoon.
4 tablespoons (liquid) . .	= 1 wineglass, or 4 ounces.
8 large tablespoons (2 wineglasses)	= 1 gill.
2 gills	= 1 breakfastcup.
1 breakfastcup . . .	= ½ pint.
2 pints (4 cups) . . .	= 1 quart.
1 cup granulated sugar .	= ½ pound.
1 cup butter (solid) . .	= ½ pound.
1 rounded tablespoon butter .	= 1 ounce.
1 heaped tablespoon sugar .	= 1 ounce.

It should be understood that all measures by cup and spoon signify that the contents of the article in question, though *full*, are *flat*, unless especially otherwise indicated by "heaped," etc. Whenever "cup" is mentioned, it means *breakfastcup*. Roughly speaking, a pint vessel holds a pound of dry material, such as sugar, flour, etc.; but this cannot be relied on with perfect accuracy.

Careful weighing and measuring is absolutely essential to success. No recipe is given a fair chance if it is carried out haphazard or by rule of thumb.

CHAPTER II

BOILED PUDDINGS

SOME GENERAL HINTS

WHERE a pudding can be steamed, it is rendered more delicate and of a better texture; but it takes longer to cook.

Such folks as do not possess even a potato-steamer can make shift with a colander placed over a pan of boiling water, and kept well covered up. No cloth is used for a steamed pudding. A piece of buttered paper is used, or paper in which butter has been wrapped (which should always be kept for this purpose).

Puddings in a mould must be put into the pan or steamer *directly* the mould is filled.

For boiled puddings in a cloth, remember to scald the cloth and wring it as dry as possible, and to flour it well in the middle before placing it under (or over) the pudding. It is best to put a plate or saucer at the bottom of the pan, lest the pudding should stick.

The slower the water for a steamed or boiled pudding boils, the better cooked the pudding will be; but it must never go off the boil.

All fruit puddings of average size (say about one and a half pounds), in basins, require boiling for not less than two hours. For steaming, about half an hour longer must be allowed. Mixture puddings of the same size, containing suet, in basins, about the same time. Puddings in cloths may be allowed a trifle less if need be.

Boiled puddings should be removed from the pan *just* before they are served up; and must not be allowed to stand about, or they will become heavy.

Be very careful to wash out and dry the pudding-cloth before putting it away. Don't leave it to go sour and unpleasant. Do not use soap to it if you can help; and dry it in the open air if possible.

All puddings containing fat or suet MUST BE PUT INTO BOILING WATER.

I. SUET CRUST, No. I

Fruit Puddings.

Shred six ounces of suet into twelve ounces of flour; mix well; add one heaped teaspoonful of baking-powder and a good pinch of salt; moisten with enough cold water to mix a fairly stiff paste (about a tumblerful should be plenty), then knead lightly and roll out once.

2. SUET CRUST, No. 2

Eight ounces of flour, mixed with six ounces of suet and eight ounces of breadcrumbs. Add one teaspoon of baking-powder and half a teaspoon of salt. Mix thoroughly, and moisten with cold water. A beaten egg is a great improvement.

Note.—Where a proportion of breadcrumbs can be used instead of all flour, great improvement is effected in boiled puddings. Half flour and half breadcrumbs is a safe rule; this applies either to " mixtures " or to suet crusts, and renders both infinitely lighter.

3. AMERICAN PUDDING

Take two large cupfuls of flour, one of chopped suet, one of golden syrup, one half-teaspoonful each of cream of tartar, carbonate of soda, and ground ginger, and a pinch of salt. A few currants or sultanas added to the above mixture will be found an improvement. If the mixture is not thoroughly moist, add a little milk, beat all together, and tie in a cloth, leaving room for swelling. Put quickly into a saucepan of boiling water, not lifting the lid for half an hour, and boil for three hours.

4. APPLE DUMPLINGS, BOILED

Peel and core the apples; have ready a soft biscuit dough (see No. 226), and either tie each apple in a separate cloth, or slice them, add sugar, and make one large dumpling. If separately, boil them fast for an hour and a half; if one only is made, two hours will be required, and the water must never stop boiling.

5. APPLE PUDDING

Six ounces of suet, one pound and a half of sliced apples, six ounces of sugar, a small pinch of salt, half a pound of breadcrumbs, half a pound of flour, and the peel of one lemon grated.   Mix these ingredients thoroughly, press into a buttered basin, which should be quite filled, and steam for four hours.

Another method is to make a suet crust with above ingredients, line a basin with it, put in the apples and sugar; place a cover of the paste on top, and tie up securely with pudding-cloth.   Boil for three hours.

6. GRANDMOTHER'S APPLE PUDDING

Take half a pound of plain flour, three ounces of suet, three ounces of cold boiled potato, a little salt, apples.   Peel, core, and cut up the apples, rub the potato in the flour (as you would butter), then add the chopped suet and salt.   Wet with a little water, and roll out on to a floured board.   Grease a pudding-basin, line it with the crust, put the apples in with a little sugar, wet the edges, and put on the top crust.   Flour a thick pudding-cloth, tie down, put into boiling water, and boil for three hours.

This can be made the day before it is wanted, and not boiled till the next day, when it will turn out a nice biscuit colour.   Can be made two days before boiling, but not longer, as the potato turns sour.   Same crust can be used for all suet-boiled puddings.

7. APPLE AND POTATO PUDDING

Boil and mash three pounds of sour apples; boil six potatoes, and add them through the masher to the apples; mix well, add half a pound of sugar, a cupful of water, and the grated rind of two lemons: one or two eggs can be added, but are not necessary. Beat well, place it in a buttered basin or mould, and steam for an hour and a half.

8. APPLE ROLY-POLY

Prepare a biscuit dough (as per No. 226); roll it thin, spread it with finely sliced or chopped apples, dust with sugar and nutmeg or cinnamon, sprinkle with bits of butter, and roll up. To be steamed for two hours, or baked in a moderate oven for one hour.

9. AUNT MARY'S PUDDING

Take a quarter of a pound each of peeled and chopped apples, raisins, currants, suet, breadcrumbs, and sugar. Mix well; add one teaspoonful of ginger and a pinch of salt; wet with milk and one egg well beaten. Steam in a buttered basin for three hours.

10. AUSTRALIAN PUDDING

Line a pudding-basin with good suet paste, then set a lemon, end up, in the bottom, in such a position that it will keep steady. Put a deep layer of well-picked sultanas around it, up to about the top of the lemon; then a layer of paste, then a somewhat thinner layer of sultanas, and so on till the basin be full (it should not be too large a one). Cover with paste, like any other boiled pudding, and steam or boil for two and a half to three hours. When cooked, turn it out upon a hot dish, and let it be cut at table with a very sharp knife, so that a little slice of the lemon goes with each helping. This is particularly good.

11. AUSTRIAN PUDDING, No. 1

A quarter of a pound of suet, one pound of flour, a quarter of a pound of sugar, one teaspoonful of baking-powder, a pinch of salt, and the grated rind of a lemon. Stir these ingredients in a basin; mix a breakfastcupful of milk with a teacupful of black treacle; stir into the flour, etc.; place in a buttered basin, and steam for three hours and a half. Turn out, and serve.

Note.—Whenever treacle has to be used, it should be warmed first.

12. AUSTRIAN PUDDING, No. 2

Mix together one pound of dried and sifted flour, two teaspoonfuls of baking-powder, six ounces of suet, two teaspoonfuls of chopped candied peel (lemon), and a tablespoonful of moist sugar. Mix a teacupful of treacle with a breakfastcupful of warm milk, stir it smoothly into the other ingredients, pour into a well-greased mould, cover with a cloth, and boil for three hours.

13. BARLEY CUSTARD PUDDING

Stew half a pint of pearl barley very slowly for four hours in one quart of milk with a little lemon-rind. It must not be stirred, but care must be taken that it does not burn. When it is done, add one tablespoonful of sugar and remove lemon-rind. Stir in one beaten egg, two ounces of stoned and chopped dates, and half an ounce of margarine. Mix thoroughly, put into a buttered mould, and steam three-quarters of an hour.

14. BARONESS PUDDING

Equal quantities of flour, suet, and stoned raisins. Mince the suet and chop the raisins, rubbing them both into the flour with a pinch of salt. Mix to a dough with milk, place in a buttered mould, cover well, and boil for four hours. This is very little inferior to plum pudding, and is both easy and quickly made.

15. BATTER PUDDING

Mix a little powdered sugar to taste, and a pinch of salt, with a half a pound of flour in a basin, then add two beaten eggs; mix them well through the flour, and gradually add one pint of milk, mixing well all the time. Should there be any lumps, they must all be made to disappear in the moistening and mixing. Let it stand a short time to rise, then butter a pudding-basin, pour the batter into it, and tie down with a cloth. Have ready a saucepan of boiling water, into which put the pudding. It must be moved about at first for a few minutes after it is put into the water to prevent the flour from falling or settling in any part. Boil the pudding for something over one hour, then turn it out, and send at once to table. Any sweet sauce you like may be served with it on the dish if liked, or in a tureen.

16. BILBERRY OR WHORTLEBERRY PUDDING

Mix one quart of picked whortleberries with one pint of flour and a pinch of salt, moistening with about half a pint of water. Tie tightly in a cloth, leaving no room for swelling; place in boiling water, and let boil fast for two hours. Serve with a sweet sauce.

17. BOLTON PUDDING

Take three ounces of flour, one ounce of butter, one ounce and a half of sugar, one egg, one small teaspoon of baking-powder, three tablespoons of milk, a little jam. Butter a basin, and place the jam at the bottom. Rub the butter in the flour; add the sugar and baking-powder; mix up with the beaten egg and milk. Pour into buttered basin. Steam for an hour and a half. Serve with sweet sauce.

18. BREAD PUDDING

Place at least one pound of stale bread to soak in sufficient warm water to cover it; when sufficiently softened, strain off the water, and add one pound of grated suet, one pound of Valencia raisins, one pound of sultanas, sugar to taste, and enough flour to bind the whole. A little golden syrup may also be used. Mix thoroughly, and either boil for two or three hours, or bake in a greased pie-dish.

19. CAROLINA SNOWBALLS

Boil some rice in milk until quite soft; prepare some large apples as for apple dumplings, and, having placed as much of the rice upon a small cloth as will entirely cover the apple like a crust, tie each up closely, and boil for two hours. Serve with melted butter and sugar.

20. CHERRY PUDDING

To two breakfastcupfuls of plain flour, add four teaspoonfuls of baking-powder, and a half-teaspoonful of salt. Moisten, stirring well, with one breakfastcupful of milk; add one breakfastcupful of ripe cherries, washed and stoned. Place the mixture in a buttered mould, and steam for not less than two hours.

21. CORNISH PUDDING

Work four ounces of dripping or lard with one pound of pastry flour, then add one pinch of salt, two ounces of sugar, and a teaspoonful of baking-powder. Beat up one egg with a little milk, grease a pudding-basin, and put an inch layer of preserve or marmalade at the bottom. Flavour the pudding mixture with lemon, and arrange on the jam so as to half fill the mould. Cover with a cloth, dipped into boiling water and floured, and steam for three hours. The pudding will quite fill the basin when cooked, and should turn out well with jam on the top. Serve with any sweet sauce.

22. CURRANT AND APPLE PUDDING

Take six large cooking apples, peeled, cored, and sliced; add the grated rind of one lemon, and four ounces of sugar. Stew till soft, add a little grated nutmeg. Have a rather rich suet crust rolled out thinly; spread it with the apple, leaving a margin all round. Sprinkle the apple with six ounces of scalded and dried currants. Roll up the pudding, being careful to secure the ends. Fasten up in a scalded floured cloth, and boil two hours.

23. DATE PUDDING

Half a pound of stoned and chopped dates, one pound of breadcrumbs, half a pound of finely chopped suet, quarter of a teaspoonful of salt, milk or water. Mix dry ingredients together, add sufficient milk or water to moisten. Put in a well-greased basin. Steam or boil from two and a half to three hours; or treat as a roly-poly, wrap in a cloth and boil for one hour and a quarter.

24. DEVON "STIR-UP" PUDDING

Take one cupful of flour, one apple cut up, one tablespoon of currants, one tablespoon of suet chopped, half a teaspoon of baking-powder, and a pinch of salt. Mix all together to a stiff paste with a little water, and steam in a basin for an hour and a half. Serve with a sauce of treacle and milk in equal parts—heated,

but not boiled. This pudding is also excellent when
made with rhubarb, gooseberries, or any sort of fruit.
The above quantities make a small pudding sufficient
for two or three persons.

25. FIG PUDDING, No. I

One pound of figs, half a pound of beef suet, half
a pound of flour, half a pound of breadcrumbs, one
egg, and about one pint of milk. Chop the suet and
figs quite small, add all the other ingredients, wet
with the egg and milk, place in a buttered basin, and
boil for three hours or steam for four. Turn out, and
serve with sweet sauce.

26. FIG PUDDING, No. 2

Mix together a quarter of a pound of flour, half a
teaspoonful of baking-powder, a pinch of salt, two and
a half ounces of grated suet, and a quarter of a pound
of cheap figs. Moisten with one teacupful of milk,
mix well, put into a basin, and boil for two hours.

27. FIG PUDDING, No. 3

Take four ounces of grated suet, four ounces of
breadcrumbs, four ounces of sugar, four ounces of
finely chopped figs, four ounces of flour, and one
teacupful of golden syrup. Mix with a little milk,
and stir in lastly one teaspoonful of baking-powder.
Pour into basin, and steam for three hours.

28. GINGER PUDDING (SPONGE)

Take six ounces of flour, three ounces of suet, one
tablespoonful of sugar, half a teaspoonful of mixed
spice, half a teaspoonful of carbonated soda, half a
teacupful of milk, half a teaspoonful of ground ginger,
two tablespoonfuls of golden syrup, and steam for an
hour and a half.

29. GOOSEBERRY PUDDING

Take one quart of green, fullgrown gooseberries, top
and tail them, scald with boiling water, and leave till
cold; drain. Rub six ounces of grated beef suet into
one pound of flour; add half a teaspoon of salt and

half a pint of very cold water. Roll out in one large round, put half a pound of sugar to the gooseberries, and place in centre of round; draw it together and tie it up, leaving room to swell. Put a plate at bottom of a pan of fast-boiling water, and place the pudding on it; boil for three hours, and reverse the pudding now and then.

30. GRAMMAR SCHOOL PUDDING

Half a pound of flour, a quarter of a pound of suet, one ounce of candied peel, half a teaspoonful of carbonate of soda; mix dry, add half a pound of treacle, a quarter of a pint of milk, and boil for one hour and a half.

31. HELSTON PUDDING

Two tablespoons each of flour, sugar, breadcrumbs, ground rice, currants and sultanas, three tablespoons of chopped suet, one tablespoon of cut candied peel, a pinch of salt. Mix up with milk in which one teaspoon of carbonate of soda has been dissolved. Boil or steam in a greased basin for two to three hours.

32. JERMYN PUDDING

Mix half a pound of flour with a quarter of a pound of suet, a quarter of a pound of shredded candied peel, one teaspoonful of baking-powder, and half a pound of treacle. Put in a basin and steam for three hours. Serve with lemon sauce.

33. LEMON DUMPLINGS

Make a soft biscuit dough (as No. 226), cut out in rounds, place one teaspoonful of lemon marmalade in the middle of each, tie up in small pudding-cloths (well scalded and dredged), and place in boiling water. Cook for forty-five minutes.

34. LEMON PUDDING

Mix two tablespoonfuls of flour, and half a pound of grated bread, or that rubbed through a coarse wire sieve; add a quarter of a pound of finely chopped suet, the grated rind and juice of one lemon, and a quarter of a pound of castor sugar, and one well-beaten egg; when well mixed, put into a buttered mould, and steam for two hours. Turn out, and pour sweet sauce round the pudding.

35. LISTER PUDDING

Take a quarter of a pound of flour, two ounces of castor sugar, two ounces of butter, one teaspoonful of baking-powder, one egg, three tablespoonfuls of milk, and a little jam. Rub the butter into the flour, add the rest of the ingredients. Take a buttered basin, and line with jam or split raisins. Put in the mixture, and steam for one hour and a quarter. Serve with white sweet sauce or jam sauce.

36. MARCH PUDDING

Three-quarters of a pound of flour, a quarter of a pound of good beef dripping or suet, a large lemon, some moist sugar, and a little salt. Rub the fat into the flour, add sufficient water to make a firm paste, roll it out on a strip half an inch thick. Strain the juice of a lemon into a cup, add the grated rind of a lemon, stir it into a teaspoonful of flour, and enough moist sugar to make it a stiffish thick paste. Spread the lemon mixture over the paste, roll it up, secure the ends, and tie in a floured cloth. Boil for three to three and a half hours or longer, if suet be used, turn carefully on to a dish, and sift sugar over.

37. MARITANA PUDDING

Take one egg, its weight in fresh (dissolved) butter, and in flour, and in breadcrumbs; add one table-spoonful of marmalade, one of raspberry jam, and half a teaspoonful of carbonate of soda. Break the egg, and beat it well; add the dissolved butter, the crumbs, flour, jam, and marmalade, and the soda last of all, stirring briskly. Butter a basin, pour in the mixture, tie it down with a buttered paper, and steam the pudding for an hour and a half. Turn out; serve with a custard sauce. This will be a dark, rich-looking pudding, as light as a feather.

38. MARMALADE PUDDING

Mix eight ounces of self-raising flour with four ounces of suet and about four ounces of sugar; add a pinch of salt; bind the whole with half a pound of orange marmalade. Pour into a buttered basin and boil for three hours.

39. OXFORDSHIRE PUDDING

Wash some rice well in several waters, and tie it up, but not too tightly, in a pudding-cloth; put it on in cold water, and let it boil for two hours. Mix some well-washed currants with the rice, and eat with sweet sauce, or cold butter and sugar.

40. PATRIOTIC PUDDING

Two ounces of flour, two ounces of butter, one ounce and a half of castor sugar, one egg, half a teaspoonful of baking-powder, half a teaspoonful of lemon juice, salt, a little milk. Cream the butter and sugar, add the beaten egg and milk alternately with the flour, lastly add the baking-powder. Put jam into the bottom of a greased basin. Pour the mixture in, and steam for one hour.

41. RIBSTON PUDDING

Mix equal quantities of breadcrumbs, chopped apple, and grated suet, with the juice and grated rind of one lemon; add sugar to taste, and steam for three hours.

42. RICE PUDDING, No. 1

Wash well in cold water three ounces of rice; drain well, then place in a saucepan with two gills of cold water, three gills of cold milk, a good saltspoonful of salt, half a saltspoonful of grated nutmeg, and two level tablespoonfuls of fine sugar. Place on the fire and boil for thirty-five minutes, mixing once in a while with a wooden spoon to prevent burning at the bottom. Pour into a hot dish, and serve with cream and fine sugar separately.

43. RICE PUDDING, No. 2

Half a pound of rice, half a pound of suet chopped fine, and a quarter of a pound of sugar. Put these ingredients in a saucepan, and boil until quite tender.

Butter a mould or basin, stick it with raisins and a slice or two of citron, pour in the rice, etc., and boil for half an hour. Turn it out of the mould or basin, and serve hot.

44. RICE BOILED TO SERVE WITH COMPOTES OF FRUIT

Blanch one cupful of rice; add salt and one quart of milk or hot water, and cook until the liquid is absorbed and the rice is tender, adding more liquid if needed. Add one-fourth of a cupful of butter, a quarter of a cupful of sugar, and, if desired, the grated rind and juice of half a lemon or one teaspoonful of vanilla extract; mix thoroughly without breaking the kernels of rice. Butter a round basin or a border mould, and press the rice into this. Set in the oven for ten minutes, then turn on to a serving-dish.

45. ROLY-POLY PUDDING

To eight ounces of flour add four ounces of suet finely grated, a good pinch of salt, and half a teaspoonful of baking-powder. Mix with a little cold water into a stiff paste. Roll out about a quarter of an inch thick, spread with jam (but not right to the edge). Moisten the edge, roll up (not too tightly), place in a well-scalded and floured pudding-cloth, fasten the ends with string, and put into fast-boiling water, which must *remain boiling* for two hours.

Note.—A layer of crumbs placed first, in making jam roly-poly, will prevent the jam oozing out.

46. ROLY-POLY, TREACLE

Mix eight ounces of flour and four ounces of suet into a paste, with as little water as possible. Roll out, and cover to within one inch of outside edges with a layer of fine crumbs; sprinkle this with the juice and grated rind of a lemon; lastly, put a layer of golden syrup. Roll up, tie in a scalded floured cloth, boil two and a half hours.

47. SPONGE PUDDING

Half a pound of flour, three ounces of sugar, three ounces of butter, one teaspoonful of ground ginger, one teaspoonful of bicarbonate of soda, one teacupful of milk; mix dry ingredients together, then rub in the butter, and add the soda (ready dissolved in warm milk); beat it to a soft batter. Steam in a buttered basin for two or three hours. Serve with sweet sauce.

48. SPOONFUL PUDDING (SEVENTEENTH CENTURY)

To one tablespoonful of flour and one tablespoonful of cream or milk, add a beaten egg, a little nutmeg, ginger, and salt. Mix all together, with a few currants if you choose, and boil it in a basin for half an hour.

49. SUFFOLK DUMPLINGS

Take one pound of dough, divide it into six equal parts, mould these into dumplings, and drop them into fast-boiling water. Boil quickly for ten to fifteen minutes, and serve them the instant they are dished. They should each be slightly torn apart with two forks, to let the steam out, directly they are taken out of the saucepan, or they will be heavy in the middle.

50. TAPIOCA (OR SAGO) PUDDING

Note.—Tapioca is obtained from the heated juice of the cassava plant; sago is the pith of a species of palm. In many respects, such as their starchy nature and gelatinous quality, they greatly resemble each other. There is both small and coarse sago; there is both plain and flaked tapioca. They can be treated in very much the same ways.

Take half a cupful of tapioca (or sago) and one quart of cold milk; let it soak in some of the milk till thoroughly steeped and softened. Place the rest of the milk in a double-boiler; add two tablespoonfuls of sugar and half a teaspoonful of salt. Put the softened tapioca to the boiling milk, and let cook till thick. A little butter is an improvement. If desired, two beaten eggs may be lightly mixed in, just before removing the pudding; flavouring to taste may also be added just at the last.

Fruit juice may be substituted for the milk, or water, or milk and water.

51. TOWN PUDDING

Six ounces of suet, half a pound of grated bread-crumbs, six ounces of moist sugar, half a pound of apples after being pared and cored, one teaspoonful of finely cut lemon rind, a small pinch of salt. Mix ingredients thoroughly, and press them tightly into a mould (well buttered); tie floured cloth over, and boil for four hours. Turn out carefully. No other moisture required.

52. SPANISH TREACLE PUDDING

Six ounces of flour, two ounces of suet, four ounces of treacle, a quarter of a teaspoonful of carbonate of soda, one gill of milk. Chop the suet, and with the hands work it into the flour; put the carbonate of soda into luke-warm milk; add the treacle to the dry ingredients; mix all with a wooden spoon, and stir in the milk. The pudding should not be stiff. Place in a greased mould, leaving room for the pudding to swell. Cover with a greased cloth. Plunge into fast-boiling water and cook steadily for two hours. As the water evaporates, put more boiling water from a kettle.

53. TREACLE SPONGE PUDDING

A quarter of a pound of flour, a quarter of a pound of suet, a quarter of a pound of golden syrup, a pinch of salt, one teaspoonful of baking-powder. Mix thoroughly, and put into buttered mould. Boil for quite two hours.

54. VERMICELLI PUDDING

Steep one cupful of vermicelli for ten minutes in sufficient boiling water to cover it (it should be covered over with a lid or plate). Add four ounces of stoned raisins, two tablespoonfuls of orange marmalade, two beaten eggs, and a little sugar; not forgetting a pinch of salt. Mix thoroughly, pour into buttered mould, boil one and a half hours; serve hot.

55. WINCHESTER PUDDING

Cut out little rounds of bread; spread them with butter and jam; put in alternate layers, with a little chopped suet, in a greased mould, till half full; add an egg whisked up with half a pint of milk.   Steam.

56. YEAST PUDDING

Mix dough as for rolls, or procure some from the baker; make it up into dumplings, and boil for about twenty minutes.   Serve with golden syrup or with sweet sauce.

57. CHRISTMAS PLUM PUDDING

Carefully remove the fibres and strings from half a pound of fresh beef-kidney suet, finely chop along with two tablespoonfuls of flour, and place in a large bowl, adding half a pound of well-picked and washed currants, half a pound of seeded grapes, a quarter of a pound of fresh breadcrumbs, two ounces of chopped candied lemon peel, half a pound of fine sugar, half a teaspoonful of ground cinnamon, one saltspoonful of grated nutmeg, half a pint of good rum, and three eggs.   Briskly mix the whole together with a wooden spoon for five minutes. Dip a piece of cloth in cold water and wring it out; spread the cloth on a table, lightly butter it with the hand, and sprinkle a little flour over it; shake the cloth to remove the excess of flour.   Place the contents of the bowl in the centre of the cloth, bring up the four corners together so as to entirely enclose the pudding, and tightly tie it all round.   Have plenty of boiling water in a large pan and plunge in the pudding.   Cover the pan, and let boil for two and a half hours.   Remove it from the water and hang up for ten minutes.   Cut the string, and carefully turn it on a hot dish without breaking.   Dredge with three tablespoonfuls of sugar, pour over one gill of rum, set it on fire, and immediately serve with a hard sauce separately.

Note.—The above pudding will be considerably more than enough for one dinner, and whatever is left over can be wrapped in a clean cloth and put away in a cold place, as it will keep in good condition for three weeks.

CHAPTER III

BAKED PUDDINGS

NOTE.—Generally speaking, baking is a treatment specially applicable to layer puddings rather than mixtures; it also imparts a peculiarly pleasant taste to milk puddings, otherwise somewhat insipid and in need of flavours from other sources. Boiled or steamed puddings stand more in need of sauces to render them attractive; but sauce with baked pudding is rather an unusual thing.

In baked puddings in which eggs are employed, one must not have too hot an oven. The same rule applies if the pudding be thickened with, or mainly composed of, ingredients which have been previously cooked— *e.g.* boiled first.

Where grains, such as rice, are used, during the earlier part of the cooking they should be several times well stirred up from the bottom of the dish, no matter whether or no a skin has formed on the surface. This will greatly facilitate the process of cooking. It is a very good plan, however, to cook grain-ingredients, such as rice, in a double-boiler first, until tender, and then finish them in the oven; this will save a lot of oven-heating. As a rule, sheer waste of heat is involved in baking puddings of this sort from start to finish.

Bread-and-butter pudding, that homely and popular dish, is often spoiled by having currants or sultanas peppered over its top. They thus become hard, dry, and detestable. They should either be placed at the bottom of the dish, or strewn among the layers of bread-and-butter. Some people turn out this pudding upside-down upon a dish, but this is a mistake, as the appetising crispness of the surface is thereby rendered soggy and sodden. It should be served as it stands— in the dish.

A piece of white paper over the top prevents a pudding from becoming too hard towards the latter end of its baking. Still better, you can cover it with another baking-dish of the same size, exactly fitting. This is a most desirable method for any baked pudding which is liable to harden, and ensures its cooking evenly all over.

A méringue cover, placed over a baked pudding, heightens its attractiveness and improves its appearance.

58. ALEXANDRA PUDDINGS

Boil six apples and mash them; add to them one ounce of butter, a pinch of salt, a breakfastcupful of breadcrumbs, two eggs well beaten, a little grated nutmeg, and half a cupful of milk. Mix perfectly; then pour into wetted cups, and bake for half an hour. Turn them out, and serve with sifted sugar over.

59. APPLE PUDDING

Butter a pudding-basin and sprinkle it thickly with moist sugar; line the basin with suet crust; fill it with slices of apple, and sugar to taste; add a pinch of salt and the juice and grated rind of one lemon. Cover the top with crust, and bake in a quick oven for two hours, or steam for three or four.

60. APPLE PUDDING (SWISS)

Butter a pie-dish, and fill it with alternate layers of stale sponge cakes, cut in half and moistened with milk, and thin slices of apples. Let the sponge cakes be at the top and bottom. Place little pieces of butter on the top sponge cakes, and bake for at least an hour.

61. APPLE BATTER PUDDING

Pare and core some apples, and put as many into a pie-dish as will stand close together. Make some batter with two tablespoonfuls of flour, three-quarters of a pint of milk, and one egg well beaten; sprinkle the apples with plenty of sugar and lemon juice; add the batter, and place immediately in a hot oven for an hour and a half, when the batter should be quite set, very light, and nicely browned.

62. APPLE CAKE PUDDING

Butter a pie-dish, and strew it thickly with grated (stale) breadcrumbs, pressing them well in round the sides. Have ready some apples which have been stewed whole in a very little water, pulped through a sieve, sweetened to taste, and flavoured with cinnamon. Fill the dish nearly, then strew one ounce of butter in little bits over the apple, and cover with breadcrumbs half an inch deep. Bake till the crumbs are a golden brown; then loosen with a knife, unmould, and sprinkle with sugar.

63. APPLE DOWDY

Take about one pound and a half of apples, slices of stale bread-and-butter, a little nutmeg, one gill of water, one gill of golden syrup, two ounces of Demerara sugar. Well butter a deep baking-tin or pie-dish; line the bottom with the thin slices of bread-and-butter; peel, core, and slice the apples and nearly fill the dish with them; grate over a little nutmeg. Now mix the syrup and water, and pour it in over the apples. Put the sugar in a layer on the top, and cover all with more bread-and-butter. Cover the top over with a tin plate or lid, and bake in a moderate oven for about two hours; then loosen the edges with a knife, put on a hot dish, and serve with sugar and cream; or it can be served in the dish it is cooked in.

64. APPLE AND RICE PUDDING (ENGLISH), No. I

Boil a quarter of a pound of rice in one pint of milk, flavoured with cinnamon. Peel and core as many apples as will stand in a pie-dish; fill with sugar, with a piece of butter on each apple; add the boiled rice, and a little more milk if not moist enough. Cover the dish over, and bake for one hour.

65. APPLE AND RICE PUDDING (FRENCH), No. 2

Boil some apples until quite tender, and some rice in a separate saucepan—in the proportion of two pounds of apples to a teacupful of rice. Butter a pie-dish, and spread the rice and apples in alternate layers (adding sugar and grated lemon rind) until the dish is full. The last layer must be rice. On this place little pieces of butter, and bake with a plate over the pie-dish for quite an hour. Can be eaten either hot or cold; if the latter, turn out, and sprinkle sugar on the top.

66. APPLE AND TAPIOCA PUDDING

Peel six apples; remove the core, and fill up the cavity with moist sugar and powdered nutmeg, and on the top of each apple put a small piece of butter. Place the apples in a pie-dish, and strew round them a small teacupful of raw tapioca, sweetened with sugar. Fill the dish with water, and let the contents bake slowly in a slack oven for two hours.

67. BAKEWELL PUDDING

A quarter of a pound of flour, two ounces of butter, a pinch of salt, a little water. Rub the butter into the flour, add the water, and mix from the centre. Do not make it too moist. Flour a board, and work the paste till quite smooth. Roll it out, and line the edge of a pie-dish with a broad band of paste. Cut the remainder into rounds with a cutter, and put them overlapping one another all round the edge of pie-dish, lifting the first so that the edge is complete. Mark each round of paste with top of paste-brush handle, and make a line with a skewer as ornamentation. Put about two tablespoonfuls of jam into bottom of pie-dish. For filling mixture take two ounces of butter, two ounces of castor sugar, two ounces of flour, one egg, one teaspoonful of baking-powder, eight drops of essence of lemon. Cream the butter and sugar together; add the egg *whole* and beat well. Mix the flour, baking-powder, and essence of lemon together, and add to the above and mix well. Put this mixture on the top of the jam in the pie-dish, and spread it with a knife, evenly covering all the jam. Bake in a good oven for half an hour.

68. BANANA PUDDING, No. I

Line the sides and bottom of a buttered pie-dish with neat pieces of bread-and-butter. Have four bananas, peeled and thinly sliced; put in a layer of these, and cover them with a layer of apricot jam. Repeat alternately until the dish is full, the top layer being bread-and-butter. Bake in a hot oven for half an hour, or until the top is brown and crisp.

69. BANANA PUDDING, No. 2

Peel and mash six bananas; mix the pulp with one tablespoonful of cornflour dissolved in half a cup of cold milk; stir in half a cup of sugar and a pinch of salt. Put a layer of this in a pudding-dish; sprinkle with fine bread or biscuit crumbs and one cup of ground or chopped peanuts. Repeat alternately in layers, till there are at least two of each; dust with sugar, and place in a moderate oven for forty minutes.

70. BARLEY PUDDING

Wash one ounce of pearl barley; soak in water all night. Put it into a saucepan, with half a pint of milk, two ounces of sugar. Let it simmer till soft. When cool, add one beaten egg. Put it into a pie-dish, and bake.

71. BREAD PUDDINGS (SMALL)

Butter well some small plain moulds, and put in each a layer of fine breadcrumbs half an inch thick, then a layer of jam, and so on till the moulds are nearly full. Beat up an egg, and add to it half a pint of milk, with sugar and flavouring to taste. Pour this very slowly into the moulds, and bake about twenty minutes. Turn out the puddings, and serve with sweet sauce.

72. BREAD-AND-BUTTER PUDDING

Put a layer of cleaned currants in the bottom of a buttered pie-dish, then a layer of thin bread and butter; repeat until the dish is full. Have ready a custard made with one pint of milk, two well-beaten eggs,

sugar to taste, and a pinch of salt. Put a small quantity
of this between the layers of bread and butter. Let
bake in a quiet oven for twenty minutes or so.

73. BREAD (STALE) PUDDING

This is an excellent method of using up hard stale
pieces, both crust and crumb. Lay them in a large
bowl or pan, pour boiling water over them, cover them
with a clean cloth, and leave them overnight. Next day
strain off all moisture, weigh, and add to two pounds
of bread half a pound of grated suet or good dripping,
half a pound of stoned raisins, four ounces of brown
sugar, a pinch of salt, a little cinnamon or nutmeg at
pleasure, and enough flour—very little will be required
—to help bind the whole. As no egg is used, a very
little warmed golden syrup will help to bind the mixture.
Bake in a greased baking-tin.

74. BROWN BETTY

Peel, core, and chop enough tart apples to make two
breakfastcupfuls; place a layer of these on the bottom
of a buttered baking-dish, and sprinkle with butter,
sugar, and powdered cinnamon; upon this place a layer of
fine breadcrumbs, and repeat in alternate layers till the
dish is nearly full; the top layer should be breadcrumbs.
Cover tightly, and place in moderate oven for forty-five
minutes; then take off cover and let brown quickly.

75. CARAMEL RHUBARB PUDDING

Mix two ounces of brown sugar with two ounces of
butter, and spread the mixture all over the inside of a
pudding-basin, thickly and evenly. Have ready a
crust made with eight ounces of flour, five ounces of
finely chopped beef suet, one teaspoonful of baking-
powder, a pinch of salt, and barely enough water to
mix it into a very dry dough. Line the basin with
this, over the butter mixture. Fill with rhubarb cut
in inch lengths, and add one tablespoonful of water
and two tablespoonfuls of sugar. Cover with the rest
of the paste, and cook for two hours in a moderate oven.
Unmould upon a hot dish, and serve.

76. CASTLE PUDDINGS

Take one ounce and a half of flour, one ounce and a half of castor sugar, one ounce of butter, one teaspoonful of baking-powder, one egg, a little milk, flavouring. Cream the butter and sugar, add the egg and part of flour, then the rest of the flour and baking-powder. Pour into cup-shaped tins. Bake for about twelve or fifteen minutes. Serve with clear arrowroot sauce or jam sauce.

77. COCONUT PUDDING

Peel and grate a coconut; take three ounces of it, and mix with four ounces of breadcrumbs, three ounces of white sugar, a slight grating of nutmeg, two beaten eggs, half a pint of coconut milk, or cow's milk. Pour into a buttered pie-dish, put shreds of butter on the top, and bake in a moderate oven. Serve on a serviette, sprinkled with castor sugar.

78. CUP PUDDINGS

Beat four ounces of butter to a cream with four ounces of castor sugar; then add to this four ounces of flour, four tablespoonfuls of milk, a small pinch of salt, and four ounces of well-washed and dried currants or sultanas, and beat these all well together. Have ready seven or eight small cups or dariole moulds, rather more than half fill them with the mixture, and bake in a good oven. Turn out, and serve with jam sauce.

79. ELIZABETH'S PUDDING

Have one pound of stale bread, one pound of stewed rhubarb, two ounces of sugar, two ounces of suet, one egg. Soak the bread in just enough milk to cover. When quite soft, squeeze dry and break up with a fork; add the chopped suet, sugar, and beaten egg. Line a greased pie-dish with the mixture. Pour in the stewed rhubarb, or any other stewed fruit sweetened. Cover with another layer of bread. Bake in a moderately hot oven for one hour and a half. Serve hot.

B—Puddings

80. FIVE MINUTES PUDDING

Take one egg, two ounces of flour, castor sugar and butter, and two teaspoonfuls of baking-powder. The butter and sugar should first be creamed together, then whisk the egg well, add the flour, and finally sprinkle in the baking-powder. Spread this mixture thinly over a well-buttered tin, and bake it in a quick oven. It should be cooked in five minutes, when it must be taken out, turned on to a sugared board, spread with jam, and rolled up at once. This is very easily and quickly made.

81. JAM ROLL (BAKED ROLY-POLY)

Mix twelve ounces of flour with one teaspoonful of baking-powder and a little salt. Rub in three ounces of good lard. Add four ounces of finely chopped or grated suet, and moisten into a paste with a very little water. Roll out, spread with jam, roll up, and place in a deep, well-greased pie-dish or baking-tin, and cover completely with another dish or tin of same size. Place in a hot oven for one to one and a quarter hours. For the first twenty minutes or so the oven must be kept very hot; after that the heat can be reduced to moderate.

82. JAM AND APPLE PUDDING

Grease a deep pie-dish. Put a layer of breadcrumbs, then a few pieces of butter, the size of a nut; cover with a layer of jam, then a layer of finely cut apples, a little sugar, and a little cinnamon. Repeat these layers until the dish is full. Bake for three-quarters of an hour in a moderate oven, and, if liked, add a little méringue of white of egg, and brown it in the oven for a few minutes. This may be used hot or cold equally well.

83. LENT PUDDING-PIES, No. 1

Mix four ounces of ground rice with two ounces of sugar; mix it smooth with a little cold milk, and add to it one pint of boiling milk. Stir in the grated rind of a lemon, a pinch of salt, and a few scalded and dried currants. Roll out the paste and fill some small greased patty-pans. Put a few currants on top and bake in a quick oven.

84. LENT PUDDING-PIES, No. 2

Take a quarter of a pound of ground rice; mix it into a smooth paste with one pint of milk, two ounces of sugar, and a few currants; add a pinch of salt and a grated lemon rind. The milk, boiling, should be poured upon the rice (mixed smooth with a little cold milk or water), and the whole then put back in the pan and boiled up. Line some patty-pans with pastry-crust, fill them three parts with the mixture, and bake for twenty minutes in a good oven.

85. LEMON PUDDING WITHOUT EGGS

Take the grated rind and strained juice of two lemons; add one cupful each of sugar, of water, and of grated raw (peeled) potato. Place in a pie-dish, spread with bits of butter, sprinkle with sugar, and bake in a good oven.

86. MACARONI PUDDING

Take two and a half ounces of macaroni, and the thinly pared rind of half a lemon; simmer until tender in one pint of milk. Remove peel, and pour into a pie-dish. Have ready two or three beaten eggs mixed with one pint of milk, a pinch of salt, and sugar to taste; pour the mixture over the macaroni, sprinkle with a little grated nutmeg; place in a moderate oven for thirty minutes.

87. MARMALADE PUDDING

Three penny sponge cakes, one egg, one pint of milk, marmalade, nutmeg and ginger are required for this. Cut the sponge cakes in halves lengthways; spread some orange marmalade on each piece and lay them in a pie-dish; beat the egg thoroughly and add the milk, beating all together; pour it over the pudding, and grate a little nutmeg and ginger over the whole. Bake for one hour.

88. MATTRESS

Take two teacupfuls of flour, two ounces of dripping or butter, one teacupful of castor sugar, one teaspoonful of baking-powder, one egg, and enough milk, with the egg, to fill a teacup. Rub the dripping into flour, add the baking-powder and sugar, and mix. Beat the egg, add the milk, and mix together. Bake on shallow tin from twenty to thirty minutes. If served hot, warm the jam before spreading.

89. NOTTINGHAM PUDDING

Peel six good apples; take out the cores and leave the apples whole; fill up where the core was taken out with sugar; place them in a pie-dish, and pour over them a light batter, prepared as for a batter pudding, and bake an hour in a moderate oven.

90. QUEEN OF PUDDINGS

Soak one breakfastcupful of breadcrumbs in one pint of new milk till quite soft; then add two beaten yolks and sugar to taste. Put in a moderate oven, and bake a light brown. Remove from oven, spread a good layer of jam on the top; whisk stiff the whites of two eggs; add to them three tablespoonfuls of castor sugar; pour this méringue over jam. Replace pudding in oven till the top just changes colour.

91. RAILWAY PUDDING

Two ounces of butter beaten with one teacupful of flour; add one teacupful of castor sugar, a small teaspoonful of baking-powder, half a teacupful of milk, and one egg. Bake for fifteen to twenty minutes on two flat tins. Spread with jam, and fold over.

92. RICE PUDDING

The usual proportions for rice pudding are two ounces of rice for every pint of milk, but if you prefer a softer and more milky pudding, only use one ounce and a half of rice. Wash and put the rice into a pie-dish, then pour the milk used for cooking it over it (the dish must not be more than half full, to allow for the swelling of the grain—indeed, an inch depth of rice will suffice for a nice milky pudding; but some folks like it much more solid), and bake in a very slow oven for about two and a half hours, being very careful to see that at no time does it cook fast. This allows the grain to become creamy and digestible, and to swell to its utmost capacity. Now lift the pudding out of the oven, and let it cool, stirring into it about two to three ounces of sugar, according to taste, to the pint of milk, a spoonful or two of cream if at hand (or mix in one ounce of butter as you lift the hot pudding from the oven), with any flavouring to taste, and then let it cook again for thirty to thirty-five minutes longer. If a richer pudding is desired, add one whole egg, or two yolks, to each pint of milk, or about half a gill of cream when sweetening the pudding.

93. LEMON RICE PUDDING

Place in a double-boiler one quart of cold milk, two level tablespoonfuls of rice, half a cup of sugar, and the grated rind of two lemons. Let cook till the rice is tender and swelled out; place in pudding-dish and bake for one hour, stirring frequently till the last quarter of an hour, when let it brown. More sugar, if required, should be served separately.

94. RAISIN RICE PUDDING

Place one tablespoonful of rice in one quart of milk, with a pinch of salt. Boil for half an hour, then place in pudding-dish with one cupful of washed seeded raisins and a little sugar. Bake for one hour, stirring often; towards the end cease stirring. Let brown slightly, and serve hot.

95. SAGO PUDDING

Take a quart of milk, and put in it six tablespoonfuls of sago or tapioca. Place it on the fire till it boils; then sweeten to taste, and let it simmer for a quarter of an hour, taking care by stirring that it does not burn; then pour it into a basin, and stir into it a little fresh butter and one to three eggs, well beaten. You may now pour it into a buttered pudding-dish, and bake for an hour.

96. VERMICELLI PUDDING

Have a quarter of a pound of vermicelli boiled till tender, in one and a half pints of milk; add two beaten eggs, three ounces of butter, three ounces of sugar, a pinch of salt, and flavouring to taste (nutmeg, ratafia, lemon, or vanilla). Have ready a buttered pie-dish and pour the mixture in; place in a moderate oven for forty-five minutes. The edges of the dish can, at pleasure, be lined with good paste.

CHAPTER IV

COLD PUDDINGS, BLANCMANGES, JELLIES, AND VARIOUS SWEET DISHES TO SERVE COLD

GENERAL REMARKS

THE method of stiffening these cold dishes is either by beaten eggs, by starchy compositions, or by gelatine.

When cornflour, ground rice, arrowroot, etc., are used, with or without whisked eggs or whites of eggs, they thicken and become firm.

When gelatine is used, if in combination with wine or with fruit juice, a simple jelly results.

Also there are certain fruit jellies produced without the addition of gelatine; their own pectin, pectose or jellifying quality providing the requisite stiffening. These are exceptionally wholesome.

Be careful to rinse out with cold water, and to leave wet, the mould employed for any starchy or gelatinous composition.

If properly made, any cold pudding should turn out of its mould without difficulty or sticking. If, however, a mild shaking will not dislodge it, plunge the mould for a moment into very hot water (not over its brim, of course), and the contents should then come out all right. If the dish to receive the pudding be placed *over* the mould, then the whole thing quickly inverted, you are likely to achieve a better result than by slithering the contents of the inverted mould upon the dish. Jellies made with isinglass or gelatine, being lighter in texture than starchy compounds, should always be released by a hot-water dip as above.

It is needless to say that all dishes intended to serve cold must be kept in a cold place.

97. ARROWROOT PUDDING

Mix half a teacupful of arrowroot with half a pint of cold milk; put one pint of milk into a saucepan with two ounces of sugar and a stick of cinnamon; pound six bitter almonds, and add them to the arrow-root and cold milk. When the milk in the saucepan boils, put the arrowroot, etc., into it, stirring all the time; boil for ten minutes, and place in a wet mould until cold.

98. BLACK CURRANT PASTEL

Make half a pint of thin syrup and add to it one pound of carefully picked ripe black currants. Stew until soft enough to pass through a sieve. Return it to pan; mix smooth one full tablespoonful of cornflour in a little cold water and stir this into the fruit. Stir well for ten minutes or so, until the mixture thickens a little. Pass into a mould that has been rinsed with cold water, and let cool. Unmould when set, and send cream or custard to table with it.

99. CHERRY BREAD PUDDING (UNCOOKED)

Cut up a stale tin loaf into half slices of bread-and-butter. Place in a pie-dish in alternate layers with stewed cherries. Leave for half an hour, then serve with custard.

100. CHOCOLATE MOULD

One pint of milk, two tablespoonfuls of cocoa, two tablespoonfuls of cornflour, two tablespoonfuls of sugar. Mix the cocoa and cornflour to a smooth paste with a little cold milk, bring the remainder to boiling point, and add the sugar, then pour slowly on the paste, stirring all the time; return to the saucepan and cook very slowly; stir all the time, as it easily sticks. Pour into a wet mould.

101. CLARENCE PUDDING

One bottle of whole currants and raspberries, a little stale cake, sponge cakes, or bread, two ounces of castor sugar. Line a plain mould or basin with neatly cut pieces of bread or cake, boil the syrup with the sugar, gently heat the fruit in it, pour gently into the mould, cover the top with cake cut in dice, and

cover with a plate with a weight on it to press it. Turn
out and serve with a good custard over it. Make the
day before using.

102. COLCHESTER PUDDING

Take one pint of milk, two ounces of tapioca, the
rind of one lemon, vanilla, two tablespoonfuls of castor
sugar, stewed fruit, custard, whites of two eggs. Put
a layer of any stewed fruit in a glass dish. Put the
milk in a clean pan on the fire, pare the lemon rind very
thinly, and put it in. Bring the milk slowly to the boil,
strain out the rind, and sprinkle in the tapioca. Simmer this very slowly in the milk till it is soft and
creamy. Keep the lid on, but stir it frequently;
then add sugar and vanilla to taste. Pour it on to
the fruit; it should be just thick enough to flow over
it nicely. If too thick, add a little more milk. Let
this get cold, then pour over a good boiled custard.
Lastly, beat up the whites of the eggs to a very stiff
froth; sweeten with the castor sugar, and add a
few drops of vanilla. Colour the froth a pale pink
with a few drops of cochineal; heap it over the top of
the custard.

103. DR. WILSON'S PUDDING

Make hot fruit juice, cut rounds of bread the size of
the mould, soak them in juice, fill the mould, put a
weight on the top, then put it on the ice or in a very
cold place; turn out, serve with whipped cream or
custard over it.

104. FAVOURITE PUDDING

Take one egg, one-third of a pint of milk, a quarter
of an ounce of gelatine, and one ounce of castor sugar.
Soak the gelatine in a small quantity of the milk, beat
the yolk of an egg, and add it to the milk with the
ounce of sugar. Bring the rest of the milk to the boil,
and pour it over the gelatine, etc.; stir well, and let
the mixture boil again. Directly it reaches boiling-
point, pour it over on the well-beaten white of egg, mix
the whole thoroughly, and pour into a mould. The

B 2—Puddings

pudding must not be stirred or shaken till cold, when it should be turned out, and it will look like a thick cream surmounted by a clear jelly.

105. FIG PUDDING

Take half a pound of dried figs, chop small, and let simmer for thirty minutes in three-quarters of a pint of water. When the fruit is nearly tender, add one dessertspoonful of sugar. Remove and cool off, then add two well-beaten yolks. Put into a pudding-dish, and bake in moderate oven till set; cover with a méringue made of the two whisked whites and two tablespoonfuls of sugar. Let brown; remove, and serve cold.

106. FRUIT PUDDING

Dip a pudding-basin or plain mould into cold water. Line it with slices of bread, fill half full of hot stewed fruit, add a thin layer of thin bread, then more stewed fruit, so as nearly to fill the basin. Cover with slices of bread and press it down with a plate and weight. Turn out next day, and serve with a custard or whipped cream round it.

107. GOOSEBERRY MOULD

Soak two ounces of tapioca in cold water for a quarter of an hour; place in a saucepan. Add one pound of ripe gooseberries topped and tailed and cooked a little, one teacupful of boiling water, half a teaspoonful of ground ginger. Let all stew together for thirty minutes; stir frequently. When the gooseberries are sufficiently tender, pour off all into a wetted mould. Serve cold.

108. ORANGE PUDDING

Take two oranges and cut up small after peeling and removing the pips. Sprinkle with two ounces of white sugar. Make three tablespoonfuls of cornflour into a batter with cold milk, and afterwards add one pint of boiling milk, stirring well meanwhile, and boil for ten minutes. When the cornflour is almost done, add to it gradually the yolks of two eggs well beaten. Pour this over the oranges, whip the whites to a stiff froth, pile high on the custard, and let just brown in the oven. Serve cold or hot.

109. PALACE PUDDING

Line a mould with angelica and cherries, fill up with finger cakes dipped in jam, and pour in hot custard over it, with a little gelatine to set it; let cool, and unmould.

110. RASPBERRY AND RED CURRANT PUDDING

Take one-third of raspberries and two-thirds of red currants; stew them with a little sugar till soft; pour off the juice. Have ready a pie-dish lined with slices of stale sponge-cake. Place fruit in centre and cover it with more cake. Place a heavy weight on top, and let stand till cold. Unmould, and having boiled down the juice with a little more sugar, pour it over the pudding.

111. RICE CREAM

Take a large heaped tablespoonful of ground rice, and rub smooth with a little cold milk. Put one pint of milk in a saucepan, sweeten, and flavour with vanilla or lemon essence. When the milk is hot, add the ground rice, and stir well until it boils. Serve cold. This is an excellent accompaniment to any stewed fruit, especially rhubarb. It can either be poured over the fruit or served alone in a glass dish.

112. ROYAL PUDDING

Make some custard; add a little gelatine and whipped cream and some brown breadcrumbs dried. Set in a mould and cool. Unmould, and serve with sauce round.

113. SAGO FRUIT MOULD

Put five tablespoonfuls of sago into cold water and let it stand all night, then strain it and mix it with one quart of currants and raspberries. Stew it till quite a jelly, and stir into it white sugar to taste, then put it into a mould to cool.

114. SAGO LEMON MOULD

Put one quart of cold water in a lined pan, with two large tablespoonfuls of sago; let soak for one hour before placing on fire. Let boil, then add a small cupful of sugar, the juice of two large lemons, and the grated rind of one. Stir well, and when it thickens and is clear and soft, remove and lightly beat in two whisked whites of eggs. Let cool. Tapioca may be used instead of sago, and milk instead of water; in the latter case, use no lemon juice, only the rind.

115. ORANGE TAPIOCA

Make a plain water tapioca (see No. 50), sugar it to taste; beat lightly into it one whisked white of egg, and pour it over peeled and sugared sliced oranges.

116. PINEAPPLE TAPIOCA

Make a plain tapioca, with half a cupful of tapioca and one quart of milk or water (as No. 50). Let cool a little, and stir in one pint of pineapple shredded (fresh) or cut into dice (tinned).

BLANCMANGES

Note.—As the word blancmange (originally *blanc-manger*, "white to-eat") explains itself, one need only remark that in many cases a so-called blancmange is merely a stiff, cold, moulded sweet dish, not necessarily white at all, but thickened with cornflour or isinglass—*i.e.*, the stiffening agent is white, even if the result is not. Care should be taken to follow out recipes exactly, and thus to achieve the happy medium between too stiff and too " sloppy."

117. ARROWROOT BLANCMANGE

Take one ounce of arrow root, if of the best quality, or four heaped tablespoonfuls of the second best, and mix it in a bowl with a little cold milk until quite smooth, with no lumps. Have ready some boiling milk, about two and two-thirds breakfastcupfuls;

add sugar to taste, and pour over the arrowroot. Return all to pan, and let boil gently, stirring with care, for three or four minutes; then stir in essence of vanilla to taste, and pour off into a wetted mould.

118. BANANA BLANCMANGE

Have ready one quart of boiling milk in a double-boiler. Add half a cupful of sugar, a pinch of salt, and three tablespoonfuls of cornflour mixed smooth in half a cupful of cold water. Let thicken, then stir in the sieved pulp of three large bananas, and one white of egg whisked stiff. Place in wetted mould, and let cool. Make the egg yolk into a thin custard to serve with this.

119. CHOCOLATE BLANCMANGE

Put one pint of milk into a saucepan over the fire; mix smooth three ounces of cornflour and two heaped tablespoonfuls of grated chocolates with one gill of cold milk. When the milk comes to boiling-point, add the cornflour; stir all the time, till it gets thick, then remove from the fire; add two tablespoonfuls of sugar and one teaspoonful of vanilla essence. Pour the mixture into a mould that has been rinsed with cold water, and turn out when firm. Fill the centre with whipped cream or méringue.

120. CORNFLOUR BLANCMANGE

Mix three heaped tablespoonfuls of cornflour quite smooth in a little cold milk. Have one quart of boiling milk, seasoned with three tablespoonfuls of sugar and a pinch of salt. Carefully pour in the cornflour, and let cook gently, stirring well, for about five minutes; then add any required flavouring to taste, such as vanilla or ratafia. (If eggs be added, either whisked whites only, or beaten yolks and whites can be used. These must be lightly beaten into the cornflour, just before pan is taken off the fire, and on no account allowed to boil.) Pour off into a wetted mould and let cool.

JELLIES

Note.—For summer use allow two ounces of gelatine to three pints of liquid. In winter, three and a half pints of liquid will be available.

Gelatine must not be allowed to heat to boiling-point or even near it. It must be always softened in cold water and added to the rest of the hot ingredients, or dissolved by setting the dish containing it in another filled with hot water.

Isinglass may be employed in place of gelatine; it is more expensive, but much more nutritious. Half an ounce to three-quarters of a pint of liquid is a common allowance, or a one-ounce packet of a good isinglass to one quart of liquid. In warm weather, a little more may be requisite.

When jellies are made of wine or of fruit juice, the flavour is better emphasised if lemon juice be employed, at the rate of one lemon per quart of jelly.

Fruit juices should not be heated, if possible, as this is apt to destroy their aroma. The only exception is pineapple juice, which must be scalded before combining with milk, eggs, or gelatine.

Jelly should be strained in a warm place, out of a draught, and then placed in a cool position. All jelly-bags or muslins should be kept scrupulously clean.

In whisking whites of eggs, add a pinch of cream of tartar when they are half done, and continue to whisk. This will ensure their remaining stiff.

121. APPLE JELLY

Peel, core, and slice one pound of good cooking apples. Place in a lined pan with half a pint of water, four ounces of loaf sugar, and the juice and grated rind of one lemon. Let simmer until tender enough to pass through a sieve. Have one ounce of gelatine softened in a little water. Return apple-pulp to pan with gelatine; let it heat through without boiling, and pour off into a mould.

122. APRICOT JELLY

Open a tin of apricots, and place them on the fire with six ounces of sugar and one pint of boiling water. Take out the apricots, and, when they have boiled two minutes, skin them. Have ready one ounce of gelatine dissolved in half a pint of water; add it to the contents of the saucepan; stir all the time, and heat through, without boiling, for five minutes. Wet a mould, lay the aprciots in it, and fill up with the liquid. Turn out when cold.

123. ARROWROOT JELLY, No. 1

Mix in a bowl one heaped tablespoonful of arrowroot quite smooth with a little cold water. Add one well-beaten egg, three tablespoonfuls of granulated sugar, and one lemon (grated rind and juice). Blend thoroughly, and pour on to the mixture enough *boiling* water to make one pint. Place in a lined pan, boil and stir for two or three minutes, and pour into wetted mould.

124. ARROWROOT JELLY, No. 2

Grind or grate three bitter almonds; put them with the peel of one lemon into a large wineglass of cold water and let steep for four or five hours. Strain off the liquid. Mix four tablespoonfuls of arrowroot smooth in some of the water, then add the rest, with four table-spoonfuls of lemon-juice and two teaspoonfuls of brandy. Sweeten to taste, and stir over the fire till it thickens. Pour off into moulds.

125. BANANA JELLY

One ounce of gelatine dissolved overnight in one pint and three-quarters of cold water; add next day the pulp of six mashed bananas, a quarter of a pound of sugar, and the juice of half a lemon. Stir well while on the fire until it boils. Place in a wetted mould.

126. BREAD JELLY

Toast some very thin slices of stale baker's bread to a light brown; stew them in as much cold water as will cover them for an hour, then beat through a sieve and place in a wetted mould. This may be flavoured with any sort of fruit, or mixed with milk or wine.

127. CIDER JELLY

Take two pints of cider and two heaped tablespoonfuls of gelatine; soften the latter in a little cold cider. Boil the rest of the cider, then add one pound of sugar and lastly the gelatine. Strain into a wetted mould, and let cool, on ice if possible. Unmould, and serve with cream or new milk.

128. COFFEE JELLY

Soak one ounce of gelatine in half a cupful of cold water. Add one cupful of boiling water and three-quarters of a cupful of sugar; let cool, add two cupfuls of clear black *freshly-made* coffee, strain, and pour into wetted mould.

129. LEMON JELLY

Soak one ounce of gelatine in half a cupful of cold water. Add two cupfuls of boiling water and one cupful of sugar. Stir until all is dissolved; when cool, add one cupful of lemon-juice. Strain through cheese-cloth and pour into mould. The thinly peeled lemon-rind may be steeped in the boiling water and withdrawn before the latter is added to gelatine. Or a little cinnamon powder to taste may be put in.

130. ORANGE JELLY

Have one ounce of gelatine soaked in half a cupful of water and proceed as for Lemon Jelly, taking care to strain the orange-juice before adding it.

131. ORANGE MACÉDOINE JELLY

Prepare Orange Jelly as above. Stand a wetted mould in very cold water. Pour in a little jelly, let it set, then arrange upon it " cloves " or " quarters " of orange with the pips removed. Dip other sections in the jelly, arrange them against the sides of the mould, and let them set; then fill up with alternate layers of jelly and orange.

132. PRUNE JELLY, No. I

Cook one pound of prunes in half a pint of water with eight lumps of sugar and the juice of half a lemon. Remove the stones and reheat the prunes; dissolve half an ounce of gelatine in a quarter of a pint of cold water, and add to fruit. Pour into a mould, and when set and cold, unmould, stick all over with split blanched almonds, and serve with a little cream.

133. PRUNE JELLY, No. 2

Dissolve one ounce of gelatine in three-quarters of a pint of water overnight. Proceed as above, with a pound and a half of prunes and one pint of water. Take out the prune stones, crack them, and place the kernels with the prunes. Mix it with the prunes, etc.; simmer together for five minutes. Place in a wetted mould.

134. PRUNE JELLY, No. 3

Wash one pound of prunes; stew them in one pint of water until quite soft. Remove stones, and pass prunes through sieve; return them to pan. Dissolve one ounce of gelatine in a little warm prune-juice, and put it to the prunes, with sugar to taste, and the juice and grated rind of half a lemon. Pour off into wetted moulds.

135. RHUBARB JELLY, No. I

Wash and cut one pound of rhubarb, stew it in a covered earthen jar, with sugar to taste, until tender enough to sieve. Add one ounce of gelatine dissolved in one breakfastcupful of water, and the juice of half a lemon. Colour with a few drops of cochineal, and pour into mould.

136. RHUBARB JELLY, No. 2

Cut one pound of rhubarb into inch-lengths, place in a baking-dish in alternate layers with sugar (one breakfastcupful will suffice). Add one cupful of cold water, the thinly peeled rind of one lemon, and a little syrup of preserved ginger or a small piece of root-ginger. Bake until the rhubarb is tender but not broken.   Remove the rind and root.   Soak one ounce of gelatine in half a cupful of cold water and stand this in hot water till it dissolves.   Strain it into the rhubarb, add juice of one lemon, and pour into wetted mould, a little at a time, letting set a little before adding more, otherwise the rhubarb will all sink to the bottom.

137. STRAWBERRY JELLY

Crush one pint of ripe strawberries, pass them through a sieve or cloth fine enough to retain seeds.   Have one ounce of gelatine softened in cold water and dissolved by standing in hot water.   Add two-thirds of a cupful of sugar and let cool; add strawberry juice and pulp, and juice of one lemon.

CHAPTER V

PANCAKES, FRITTERS, SWEET OMELETS, AND CROQUETTES

Note.—Pancakes, Fritters, and Omelets are by no means the same thing. All are made of batter, and all are fried; but the pancake and omelet are fried in as little butter (or other fat) as possible, and the fritter in deep, boiling fat. The pancake needs to be turned; the omelet requires to be folded over; the fritter is fished out with a skimmer or strainer when cooked a crisp golden-brown. The time-honoured and immemorial tossing of pancakes, which still serves to celebrate Shrove Tuesday, is obsolete with the modern cook; she makes her pancakes small and dainty enough to be turned with a knife, and of texture good enough not to break in the process. There was formerly a great deal of waste involved in tossing, unless one had the deftest of eyes and hands.

The principal points to bear in mind with these fried puddings are (1) the frying-pan, (2) the batter, (3) the fat.

(1) An omelet-pan, specially reserved for this purpose, is best; it should be perfectly clean, and well warmed before the butter or good lard for frying is put into it. After use, wipe it carefully with pieces of paper till the paper comes away perfectly clean. If you are obliged to take a pan that has been used for something else, rub it well, first with salt, then with paper; then put a lump of dripping in, and heat this till it smokes hard and browns, when it should be poured off and the pan cleaned with pieces of paper as above described. A new pan must also be treated thus. These precautions may appear over-fastidious to the amateur, but they make all the difference between delicacy and coarseness in the pancakes, etc. A wide

frying basket is most useful for croquettes and beignets, and if of very fine mesh, for fritters.

(2) (*a*) The batter must be perfectly smooth; and it should be beaten thoroughly well *before* all the liquid is added, as it is easy to get a thick batter quite smooth, and very difficult as regards a thin one. (*b*) A batter containing few eggs requires more thickening of flour than one containing many eggs. (*c*) It should stand *at least* an hour before using; but (especially in cold weather) if it stands many hours, or even overnight, so much the better. Very few people realise the importance of this rule. (*d*) If the whites are beaten separately to a stiff froth, do not add them to the other ingredients until the very last moment, then stir them lightly in. (*e*) If a few grains of salt be added to the eggs, they can be beaten faster. For a light texture a wire whisk is best to use; for a closer one, a Dover egg-beater (wheel with handle).

(3) The best fat to use for pancakes is good butter, and as so very little is required, it is worth while to employ it if possible. Butter also is required for omelets. For fritters and croquettes, which need a deep bath of boiling fat, lard, clarified beef dripping, or olive oil, are available. It must be *boiling* when the batter is put in—*i.e.*, blue smoking. So long as this fat does not become over-heated, smoked, or burned, it may, with care, be used over and over again. (Olive oil is less apt to burn than lard or dripping.) When required again, let the fat heat through very slowly at the back of the stove, and then put in some thin slices of potato, which will clarify it by absorbing all impurities. Remove any particles or crumbs that may have been left in, or they will darken the fat and prevent it cooking properly.

Remember that when you have finished frying your first lot of fritters, etc., the fat is probably not so hot as when you put them in; therefore boil it up again to blue smoking point before putting more in.

PANCAKES

Pancakes should be dished up quite light, crisp, and free from fat; a sodden, flabby, greasy, leathery pancake is not only unappetising, but indigestible. They should not be placed one on top of another, but daintily rolled up and lightly dredged with castor sugar. Cut lemon and castor sugar are usually served along with them.

All eggs used for the purpose should be fresh and well beaten; in some instances (see following recipes), it is best to whisk the whites and yolks separately.

THREE GOLDEN RULES FOR PANCAKES

(1) Don't make them too large; from a wineglassful to a teacupful is plenty.

(2) Don't put too much butter in the pan; about the size of a hazel-nut should do *if the pan is properly clean.*

(3) Don't let the butter get too hot before putting in the batter. Directly it smokes is the right moment.

GENERAL RECIPE FOR PANCAKES

Put half a pound of flour into a basin; make a bay in the centre with your knuckles, and into this drop the yolks of two unbeaten eggs and a tablespoonful or so of milk. Stir the flour down gradually into this small pond, adding a little more milk by degrees as you work it all together, being careful not to thin it too quickly, but to keep it stiff enough to enable you to rub out any lumps, and to keep it all perfectly smooth. When you have used about half a pint of milk, beat the mixture well with a perfectly clean wooden spoon till it is a mass of air bubbles, then work in the rest of the milk—about half a pint—as before, and *let the batter stand for an hour at least*, two hours if possible, before using. Just at the last add in, quickly and lightly, the stiffly whipped whites of the two eggs. If a richer batter is desired, use four yolks and a tablespoonful or so of cream instead of the milk in the first place, and use rather less milk. Do not use more than two whites, for with too many whites the pancakes are apt to be tough. Have ready a perfectly clean pan. Melt a piece of butter the size of a hazel nut, and when it smokes, pour quickly into the very centre of the pan a wineglassful or so of batter; then, if the fat is at the right temperature, the batter will spread all over the pan directly, whereas, if it has not reached the proper heat, the pan will probably require to be tilted to get the batter to cover it properly. It must be left undisturbed for a minute or so, until it is set enough to allow the blade of a knife to be slipped under it to loosen it from the pan. Directly the under side is delicately browned, turn the pancake with the knife and brown the other side; then slip it out of the pan, strew sugar over the side last done, roll up the pancake, and keep it hot, whilst you cook the rest in exactly the same manner.

PLAINER PANCAKES

138. AMERICAN PANCAKES

Mix half a pint of Indian meal with one quart of buckwheat flour. Make a " well " in the centre, put in four tablespoonfuls of yeast, and enough warm water to moisten all into a thin batter. Beat well, put in a warm place to rise, covered with a cloth. When it has risen sufficiently and is all over bubbles, cook three cakes at a time in a greased griddle or pan. They must be browned each side. Serve very hot with treacle separately.

139. APPLE PANCAKES

Prepare a pancake batter. Peel and core two medium apples cut in quarters, then finely slice them. Heat half an ounce of good butter in a frying-pan; add apples with half a teaspoonful of vanilla essence and one tablespoonful of powdered sugar; toss them well and place in batter; mix well, and proceed to make and serve the cakes as per general recipe above.

140. CANADIAN PANCAKES

Take one pint of rye-meal, add a pinch of salt, and use enough lukewarm milk to make a thin batter. Beat well for several minutes, then add one gill of yeast. Let the mixture rise, then pour it into the pan, enough at a time to make a cake about the size of a breakfast-plate. Let the pancakes be nicely cooked both sides, butter them on one side only, and serve very hot.

141. ENGLISH PANCAKES

Make a batter with four ounces of flour, two eggs, and a little over half a pint of milk. Mix a pinch of salt into the flour, add the eggs one at a time, each with a teaspoonful of milk, and mix well; then add the rest of the milk, stirring continually. Let the batter stand one or two hours before frying.

142. GEORGETTE PANCAKES

Prepare a plain pancake batter. Cut out crosswise, from a small pineapple, six slices as thin as possible; cut each slice in eight equal pieces, and add them to the batter; then proceed, dredging a teaspoonful of fine sugar over each pancake before serving.

FRITTERS

Note.—Fritters, as already stated, must be fried, not in a mere scrap of butter like pancakes, but in a deep bath of boiling fat, like rissoles or croquettes. The fat, when the fritters are put in, should be at a temperature of 380 degrees; you can test it as follows. Drop a small piece of bread (crumb) in and count thirty; if the fat is the right heat, the bread should be brown by then, and large bubbles should be sizzling round it. Two or three fritters can be cooked at the same time; but do not put in more, or they will chill the fat. A dessertspoonful of butter should be enough for each. Fry it till it becomes a delicate golden-brown, quite light and crisp; remove with a strainer, and place to drain on paper in a hot dish; keep hot till the rest are done. Be sure the fritters are crisp and well-drained. Do not let them touch each other while draining on paper (which should be at the mouth of the oven), or you will spoil their crispness.

A pancake batter, made a trifle more liquid, can also be used for fritters.

143. BATTER FOR FRITTERS

Make a batter with one egg, one tablespoonful of flour, and enough new milk to mix it to the consistency of thick (single) cream. Let it rest an hour, or two hours if possible; just before using, beat it up again lightly. Have ready a deep pan of boiling fat, and having tested it as above, drop, or rather slide the batter in very gently, and proceed as already explained.

144. APPLE FRITTERS

Peel six large apples; core, and cut them in rings. Grate some lemon peel and mix it with moist sugar; lay every slice in this first, and then in batter (two tablespoonfuls of flour to half a pint of milk), and fry in lard for about ten minutes. When nicely brown on each side, drain them, and serve very hot, with castor sugar sifted over.

145. BANANA FRITTERS, No. 1

Prepare a batter for fritters. Cut six peeled, sound bananas in two crosswise pieces, roll them in the batter, then plunge in boiling fat and fry for ten minutes, turning with a skimmer once in a while; lift up, thoroughly drain on a towel, and neatly trim all round. Place on a hot dish, dredge a little powdered sugar on top, and serve.

146. BANANA FRITTERS, No. 2

Peel slightly under-ripe bananas, and leave one hour in a deep dish, sprinkled with lemon juice, sugar, and the grated rind of one orange (this last is not absolutely essential). Halve them lengthwise, dip each in fritter batter, and fry brown in deep fat. Drain, dust with sugar, and serve.

147. ORANGE FRITTERS

Make a plain batter; dip into this sections of orange clear of all skin, pips, and core. Fry at once in deep, boiling fat until brown; then drain, dredge with castor sugar, and serve at once.

SWEET OMELETS

Note.—These are broadly divided into two classes, " French " and " puffy." Either of them may be used as the foundation for a sweet omelet, but the " puffy " kind lends itself best to that purpose.

There are two special precautions necessary in making an omelet. (1) Not to have too much white of egg in, or the omelet will inevitably be hard. The yolks should, by good rights, be double the number of the whites, although in most recipes they are given as equal. (2) A very thin pan : because the omelet must be cooked very quickly indeed, so that the eggs are barely set. The pan should not be large, as a good omelet is small and thick.

A French omelet is made thus : Break your eggs into a bowl, add one tablespoonful of water for each egg, counting two yolks as one whole egg. Put in a pinch of salt. Beat the eggs with a fork, until a spoonful can be taken up; then strain into another bowl. Have ready one tablespoonful of butter, just melted, in a very thin, smooth, and clean pan. Pour in the batter; place it for a moment on a hot part of the range, just to let the eggs set; then, with a thin knife, separate the cooked part from the sides of the pan, and gently rock the pan to and from you, so that the part still uncooked may run down next to the hot pan. When it is creamy throughout, roll it over, beginning at the side of the pan next the handle, and keeping it a moment or two on the hot stove to brown slightly.

For French omelet made as above, the correct formula would be : Two whole eggs, two yolks, three table-spoonfuls of water, a pinch of salt, and a tablespoonful of butter (for frying). This would be termed a three-egg omelet.

A puffy omelet is made as follows : Beat the yolks until they are light-coloured and thick; beat the whites till stiff and dry. Add to the yolks one tablespoonful of cold water for each yolk, and a pinch of salt. Mix together thoroughly, then place yolks on beaten whites, and cut and fold the whites well into the yolks. Have ready the pan hot and buttered; spread the mixture evenly in.   Let stand about two minutes over a moderate heat; then set in the oven, pan and all, to cook the top slightly.   As soon as a knife thrust into the centre of the omelet will come out nearly clean, remove the pan from oven, cut the omelet across the centre of the top, at right angles to the handle (but do not cut it right through), fold the part nearest the handle over the other part, and place on a hot dish.

Omelets must be served *at once*; if they are left sticking about on racks or in ovens, they will inevitably become tough, hard, or flabby.   If you want an omelet that be can kept hot a little while, it is necessary to add a little thickening of flour, allowing, say, two table-spoonfuls to five eggs; this must be made into a white sauce with one breakfastcupful of milk and two table-spoonfuls of butter, and the separate beaten yolks and whites gradually added.   Cook as a puffy omelet.

148. FORMULA FOR SWEET OMELET

Take two fresh eggs; divide the yolks from the whites; stir the yolks a minute or two with a teaspoonful of castor sugar and a little vanilla essence.   Whip the whites stiffly; add carefully warmed butter.   Stir until beginning to set, then put into the oven to finish cooking; spread with slightly warmed jam and fold over; serve very hot.

149. APPLE OMELET

Prepare a plain omelet, and when it is enough cooked to fold, place some finely minced raw apple or some smooth stewed apple (a breakfastcupful of either) on half of it; fold the other half over and serve at once.

CROQUETTES

Note.—Croquettes are apple-, pear-, or ball-shaped; they are a fair size, about that of medium apples, pears, or peaches.   They do not fundamentally consist of batters, but of various farinaceous mixtures; and are cooked, like fritters, in deep boiling fat.

150. APPLE CROQUETTES

Take one pint of tart apples, peeled, cored, and sliced. Stew them with one dessertspoonful each of water and butter; mash smoothly; put into double boiler and let cook till the juice is nearly dried. Mix smooth one-third of a cupful of cornflour with a very little water, add a pinch of salt, mix well with the apple, and cook for a quarter of an hour. Last of all, thoroughly beat in one whisked egg. Place in a (wetted) deep dish and let cool. Then drop teaspoonfuls of this into fine breadcrumbs, dip into beaten egg, crumb again; and fry in deep boiling fat. These may be served either with sugar or with salt.

151. PORTUGUESE FRITTERS

Have ready some rounds of rather stale bread, half a dozen or so, barely half an inch thick, and one egg beaten well with a slight flavouring of vanilla or lemon and a little sugar. Mix it with about half a pint of milk. Soak the rounds of bread for *two hours* in the mixture, and fry well; put a little jam on each piece, and send hot to table.

152. SUSSEX PANCAKES (SEVENTEENTH CENTURY)

Take some very good pie paste made with hot lard and roll it thin; fry it in butter, and serve it with beaten spice and sugar as hot as you can.

CHAPTER VI

CREAMS, CUSTARDS, JUNKETS, AND TRIFLES

NOTE.—Although these delightful preparations are invariably eaten cold, they cannot be considered to come under the head of cold puddings such as are inserted in Chapter IV. They occupy a place of their own in the culinary kingdom.

Custards of the authentic species contain nothing but eggs and milk, sweetened and flavoured, with the inevitable pinch of salt not forgotten. Second-class custards are thickened with flour or cornflour, and fewer eggs are used.

Firm custards are left to cook standing in a jar in hot water (or a double-boiler), without being stirred at all. *Liquid* custards are stirred continuously. In either case, the water should not boil : the eggs should set smoothly, and a " firm " custard should appear rather firm if you touch the centre. Remember that all custards solidify a little when cool.

Eggs for custard should not be beaten too much, as they are intended to thicken and enrich, not to make the mixture lighter. One egg to each breakfastcupful of milk is a fair average proportion; but if you want a firm custard that can be turned out of a mould, you must double that number of eggs. Whole eggs can be used, or yolks only; the latter will produce the richest custard, and for a " liquid " custard are far the most advisable. (Count two yolks as one egg.) The whites, however, whisked very stiff, may be added just at the last when the liquid custard is cold. The flavouring should also be added then—not during the cooking of the custard, as is frequently and mistakenly done.

Junkets are simple, wholesome, and a very nice change from milk puddings. They need not necessarily be enriched with whipped cream. For ordinary use, a little sugar and cinnamon, or grated nutmeg, or vanilla, is sufficient to make them extremely palatable; it is their peculiar curd-like texture which makes them so particularly pleasant. The great point in making junket successfully (with essence of rennet or with junket tablets) is (1) to have good rich new milk, (2) not to let it overheat. When it reaches "bloodwarm" temperature, 98° to 100° Fahrenheit, is the right time to add the rennet; and then let the milk remain in a warm room till it sets; do not put it away in a cold pantry.

153. ARROWROOT CREAM (PLAIN)

Mix two tablespoonfuls of arrowroot with about half a pint of water; when it has well settled, pour the water off. Boil two quarts of milk, seasoned, and add the peel of a lemon and some cinnamon. Strain it, boiling, over the arrowroot, stirring it well and frequently, till cold. It is served to eat with preserved fruits or fruit tart.

154. COFFEE CREAM

One pint of milk and cream mixed, half a cupful of strong coffee added, sweeten to taste. Dissolve one ounce of gelatine (previously soaked). Beat all together, and turn into a wet mould.

155. RICE CREAM (PLAIN)

Soak some rice all night. Boil it three hours, changing the water several times, putting cold water when changed. Strain and wash. Whip cream separately, and stir together lightly. Barley is very good done the same way.

156. CUSTARD

One pint of milk, to which add two large eggs (yolks and whites), one ounce of sugar, and a little nutmeg. Beat all together in a basin with a whisk for five minutes or less, put it into a saucepan, and stir it over a clear fire till it thickens. Put into a jug half a teaspoonful of almond flavouring, then strain the custard into the jug, then again strain it into another, and keep on pouring from one jug to another till it is cold. This quantity will make twelve excellent custards, or it may be served in a glass dish.

157. CHEAP CUSTARD

Boil one pint of milk, sweeten it with any spice you like. Rub smooth two tablespoonfuls of ground rice in a little cold milk, then put into it two yolks of eggs well beaten. Afterwards add the boiled milk, and stir them well together; then stir it over a slow fire till it thickens, but it must not boil.

158. JUNKET

Crush one junket tablet, and dissolve in one tablespoonful of cold water (or use essence of rennet, two teaspoonfuls to a quart of milk). Have one quart of new milk, with a little sugar in, warmed to blood-heat (98 degrees), stirring constantly; add one teaspoonful of vanilla and two to four teaspoonfuls of rum, brandy, or sherry; stir in the junket tablet (or essence of rennet), and let all become evenly mixed. Pour into a large bowl, and let stand in a warm room until it sets like a jelly; then move it into a cool place, being careful not to shake it. Immediately before serving, dust the top with (mixed) powdered sugar and cinnamon or nutmeg. Before doing this, the top may be covered with whipped or clotted (Devonshire) cream.

159. COFFEE JUNKET

To one pint of new milk add half a teacupful of strong coffee and one dessertspoonful of castor sugar. Make as you would ordinary junket, using one teaspoonful of essence of rennet or one rennet tablet. Pour into the bowl it will be served in, and let it stand in a moderately cool place till set. Whip some cream with a little sugar, and arrange it in little knobs on the top of junket. Leave cream till just before it is sent to table.

160. APRICOT TRIFLE

Open a tin of apricots, warm the syrup, add sugar if necessary, then put in the apricots and cook a few minutes. Cut stale sponge cakes into slices, and place in glass dish; pour a little warm apricot syrup over them, and leave quite an hour. Put apricots (peaches or pears, half a tin) on the sponge cake, then a custard. Finish the top with whipped cream, sweetened and flavoured (a whipped white of egg may be added to make more of it); decorate with pistachio nuts, cherries, or angelica. For each requisite pint of custard allow half a pint of milk, one egg (a yolk of another egg may be added), one ounce of loaf sugar, and one teaspoonful of corn-flour.

161. COUNTESS TRIFLE

Cut five sponge cakes in half. Place on a dish with alternate layers of fruit, the last layer being fruit. Make a nice thick custard, and flavour with orange-flower water; sweeten to taste, and when nearly cold pour it over the fruit.

162. CHESTNUT TRIFLE

Take one pound of chestnuts, slit each, cover with cold water in a saucepan, bring to the boil and let boil five minutes. Let stand in the hot water (moving pan off fire) for ten minutes, then take off the shells and skins. Place in a lined pan only just covered with milk and simmer until soft enough to sieve. Put in sugar and vanilla to taste, also a minute pinch of salt. Pile up the purée in a glass dish and dust all over with cocoa powder or grated chocolate. When quite cold, pour a custard round it.

163. PEAR TRIFLE

Take a tin of pears, and empty it carefully into a glass dish; put in as little syrup as possible. Make some raspberry jelly (a pint packet will suffice), and pour most of it over the pears, but keep back a little. When this is cold and firm, pour a pint of custard over it (which can be made with custard powder), and let that also get cold. Whisk some cream stiff, sweetening it with a little castor sugar, and pile it on top of the custard. Decorate with strips or cubes of the remaining jelly.

CHAPTER VII

FRUIT DISHES

NOTE.—Under this heading are included such sweet dishes as are made almost entirely of fruit—fresh or dried, cooked or uncooked—with very little, if any, addition of other materials.

These dishes are among the most important and wholesome that can be set upon the table. They are of immense variety; and indeed, to a large extent, they depend upon the housewife's skill in ringing the changes upon different methods. The formula prescribed for one fruit will, with the most trifling alterations, usually be found available for another. Hence, if recipes for certain fruits are found less numerous than for others, it is because space and scope do not allow, nor is it necessary to recapitulate recipes which will serve equally well for most fruits of similar kinds.

The reader will realise that it has been by no means easy to discriminate one fruit dish from another, and to decide what should by rights figure here, and what in Chapters II and III. She will find, however, that hardly anything is inserted in this chapter which could conveniently figure as a *pudding* baked or boiled.

The value of fruit extends far beyond its nutritive qualities (which, in the case of figs, dates, raisins, currants, nuts, and bananas are very great). It contains also, salts and organic acids, which are most beneficial to the blood; and provides a variety of flavours and of textures which we can hardly imagine ourselves without.

Remember never to use an iron spoon in stirring fruit while cooking; only a wooden or a silver one. Remember also, that the less water you use, the better the flavour and appearance of the fruits will be.

If sugar be scarce, honey is the best substitute as regards fruit; dates may be considered second-best, especially for sweetening rhubarb. " Corn syrup " and glucose may also be employed.

164. APPLE AMBER

Take a strip of rough puff pastry, one pound of apples, two ounces of butter, two ounces of sugar, two eggs, two ounces of breadcrumbs, a little grated lemon rind. Line the sides of a pie-dish with the strip of pastry, decorating the edge. Peel, core, and cut up the apples. Stew these until quite tender; add the sugar, butter, breadcrumbs, and yolks of egg. Place this mixture in the pie-dish, and bake for half an hour. Beat up the whites stiffly, and two tablespoonfuls of sugar. Pile this méringue on top of the apple mixture, and set slowly in a cool oven. Decorate with cherries and angelica. Apple amber is excellent hot or cold.

165. APPLES BAKED, No. 1

Wipe nicely, and core with an apple-corer, six fine, sound, not too ripe apples. Lay them in a tin with half a gill of hot water. Fill the cavity of each with granulated sugar, and baste the top of each with just a little melted butter. Place in a moderate oven for thirty-five minutes, or until nice and soft. Remove from the oven. Dress on a hot dish, and serve with a pitcher of cream or milk.

166. APPLES BAKED, No. 2

Peel and core some sound, good-sized apples. Place in a deep baking-pan, allowing one full tablespoonful of sugar and half a breakfastcupful of water to every apple. In the cavity of each place a teaspoonful of finely chopped nuts and a shred of lemon peel; dust with cinnamon and nutmeg. Let bake very slowly : a jelly will form round the fruit. A little butter and honey may be substituted for the nuts.

167. APPLES BAKED (WITH ALMONDS), No. 3

Core and pare six or eight tart apples; let simmer in a cupful each of sugar and water boiled together,

C—Puddings

two or three minutes until nearly tender. Turn the apples often to avoid breaking. A little lemon juice added to the syrup will improve the flavour, or, if the apples be rubbed with the cut side of a lemon, it will help to keep them white during the cooking. Set the apples in a lined pan, and press almonds into them, blanched and split in halves. Dredge with powdered sugar, and brown in the oven. Serve hot with jelly, or whipped cream, and the cold syrup in which the apples were cooked.

168. APPLES AND BREADCRUMBS

Peel and slice some good baking apples; place them in a pie-dish with sugar, lemon juice, and a very little butter and water; on the top of the apples sift some breadcrumbs thickly, and put a few dabs of butter on the crumbs. Bake for an hour in a brisk oven.

169. APPLES BUTTERED

Take some middle-sized apples; peel and core, but do not divide them, and put them on little round slices of bread. Put in the cavity of each apple as much butter and sugar as it will hold. Cook them in a good oven on a buttered tin, and before serving put a teaspoonful of red currant jelly in each apple.

170. APPLES WITH VANILLA BUTTER

Peel three large, sound, green apples; cut in halves, remove the cores, then cut each half in four slices. Place in an earthen baking-dish, arranged in the form of a crown, one overlapping another; sprinkle with two tablespoonfuls of castor sugar, and drop two teaspoonfuls of vanilla essence evenly over them. Divide half an ounce of good butter in small bits over the apples; cover with a lightly buttered piece of white paper. Place in a hot oven to bake for fifteen minutes or till soft; remove, place in a heated dish, pour the liquor over, and serve.

171. APPLE CHARLOTTE

Pare and slice four or five times as many apples as will fill the dish in which the charlotte is to be made.

Steam these until tender; then add sugar to taste and a generous piece of butter, and cook the apples over the fire, stirring meanwhile, until they are *very* dry. Prepare sippets of bread an inch wide, by removing crust and dipping in melted butter; with these line a plain mould, making one sippet overlap another. Arrange lozenges of bread similarly in the bottom of the mould; turn in the apple, piling it high on the top, then cover with buttered bread. Bake for half an hour in a hot oven. Turn from the mould on to a hot dish. Serve with sugar and cream or hot sauce.

172. APPLE CHARLOTTE (FRENCH)

Butter a pie-dish; cover the bottom and sides of it with thin slices of buttered bread; peel and slice some apples, lay them on the bread with some sugar and the juice of a lemon; cover them over with thin slices of bread buttered on both sides, and bake in a hot oven for an hour. To be eaten either hot or cold : if the latter, turn it out of the pie-dish and sift sugar over it.

173. APPLES AND DATES

This is a good way of utilising poor or unripe apples. Stew them partially, then measure, and to every quart of fruit add at least half a breakfastcupful of stoned and chopped dates. Let simmer for about seven minutes, then cool. A little grated lemon rind is an improvement; this should be added at the beginning.

174. APPLE DOWDY

Take one pound and a half of apples, thin slices of stale bread-and-butter, a little nutmeg, one gill of water, one gill of golden syrup, two ounces of Demerara sugar. Well butter a deep baking-tin or pie-dish. Line the bottom with the slices of bread-and-butter. Peel, core, and slice the apples and nearly fill the dish with them. Grate over a little nutmeg. Now mix the syrup and water; pour it in over the apples. Put the sugar in a layer on the top, and cover all with more bread-and-butter.   Cover the top over with a tin plate or lid, and bake in a moderate oven about two hours; then loosen the edges with a knife, put on a hot dish, and serve with sugar and cream; or it can be served in the dish it is cooked in.

175. APPLE FOOL

Boil some apples whole in as much water as will float them; pass through a sieve; add sugar and lemon juice to taste, and mix with one pint of hot milk.   To be eaten cold.

176. APPLES FRIED

Peel and core three large, good, sound apples.   Slice them into pieces half an inch thick.   Dip in cold milk, then roll them in flour.   Melt half an ounce of butter in a frying-pan.   Place the apples in the pan, and fry on a brisk fire until a nice golden colour on both sides, or two minutes for each side.   Remove them with a skimmer, and dress on a hot dish.   Sprinkle with a little powdered sugar, and serve.

177. APPLES GRILLED

Peel and core four good-sized, sound apples; trim both ends, then cut each apple in three even slices. Lightly oil a double-broiler, arrange apples on it, and broil over a brisk fire for three minutes on each side; remove, sprinkle a very little powdered sugar over, dress on a hot dish, and serve.

178. APPLES WITH JUNKET

Have ready apples cooked in syrup, or baked until tender.   Place in separate dishes, and sprinkle with chopped almonds.   Heat a pint of fresh milk, to which one-third of a cup of sugar has been added, until luke-warm, then stir into it half a junket tablet, crushed and dissolved in a tablespoonful of cold water; add a few drops of vanilla extract, and pour into the dish around the apples, which should have been cooled.   The milk will jelly when cold.   Garnish with candied cherries and whipped cream.

179. APPLES WITH RICE

Blanch one cupful of rice, then cook in boiling salted water until tender, adding more water as needed. When done, the water should be absorbed and the kernels of rice distinct. Line small buttered cups with the rice; fill the centres closely with slices of apple, cooked until tender, but not broken, in sugar and water; cover the apple with more rice, rounding the top slightly. Let steam or cook in the oven, standing in a dish of hot water about fifteen minutes. Turn out the cups on to a serving-dish, and serve hot with a cold boiled custard, made of a pint of milk, the yolks of four eggs, half a cupful of sugar, and a few grains of salt. Mock cream, hard sauce, banana sauce, or lemon sauce may be substituted. To prepare the apples, proceed as follows : Neatly peel and core six medium apples. Place them in a saucepan, and boil in two quarts of water with half a stick of vanilla and four ounces of sugar for thirty minutes. Remove very carefully with a skimmer, without breaking them, and place upon the rice. Take up the vanilla bean and put it in sugar to keep for other purposes.

180. APPLES, RUSSIAN

Take six large cooking apples; peel and core them; stuff the centre with mincemeat. Place in a slow oven and bake for two and a half to three hours. When the apples are cold, serve them, dusted with castor sugar.

181. APPLES STUFFED

Take good sound largish apples, not too sour. Peel and core them. Stuff the hollows with a few currants, one or two cloves, and ground or grated nuts of any kind. Place in a tin, with a very little water to prevent them sticking; put a tiny bit of butter on top of each apple; bake till quite tender. Make a syrup of a quarter of a breakfastcupful each of sugar and boiling water; let thicken, place apples in a dish, and pour syrup over them.

182. APPLES STEWED, No. 1

Peel, core, and slice six apples; put the parings into one quart of water, and simmer gently for half an hour; strain the liquor, and put the apples into it, with a quarter of a pound of sugar and the juice of half a lemon; boil until the apples are clear and soft; take them off the fire, and beat them up with a large cupful of milk. When quite cold, serve with whipped white of egg on the top.

183. APPLES STEWED, No. 2

Take sound apples, wipe well, and place in a lined pan with just enough water to prevent them sticking. Cook till tender enough to pass through a sieve; then sweeten to taste while they are still warm enough to dissolve the sugar. This is an economical method (always practised on the Continent), as nothing is left except the pips; the pulped skin also imparts a particularly good flavour to the apples.

184. APRICOT CHARLOTTE

Soak half a pound of dried apricots overnight in sufficient cold water to cover them when expanded. Next day, stew them until quite soft, and rub through a sieve. Butter a plain mould or pie-dish, line the bottom with thin slices of bread-and-butter, and put in a layer of apricot pulp, sprinkled with sugar to taste. Repeat until the dish is full up; the last layer should be bread-and-butter. Put into a good oven for about fifty minutes. Turn out upon a heated dish, and sprinkle with castor sugar; serve hot.

185. BANANAS, BAKED, No. 1

These may be treated in various ways, as follows. The bananas may either be baked whole in their skins, one strip being pulled back, or peeled and halved lengthways. In the latter case, put them in a baking-tin containing half a cupful of sugar, little bits of butter, a pinch of salt, and a sprinkling of cinnamon. Lastly, pour in half a cupful of water. Bake in a quick oven. Or pour over the fruit a syrup made of lemon juice, water, sugar, and butter. Or place some peeled, cored, and halved apples along with the bananas, and flavour by either of above methods.

186. BANANAS, BAKED, No. 2

Peel and cut six bananas in half, lengthwise, and place in a baking-dish. Mix on a plate half an ounce of fresh butter, one ounce of sugar, and six drops of vanilla essence. Spread this mixture over the bananas evenly, and set in the oven for ten minutes, being careful to baste them once in a while with their own liquor. Remove and serve.

187. BANANAS, BAKED, No. 3

Select rather green bananas, put them entire into hot ashes, or a very hot oven, and bake until the skins burst open. Serve at once, in a folded napkin, with butter.

188. BANANAS, BAKED, No. 4

Lay in a pie-dish some ripe bananas, peeled but not cut up. Sprinkle them with a little lemon juice and sugar, half cover them with water, and bake for twenty minutes. When they are cool, serve with custard, cream, or milk.

189. BANANA CUSTARD

Take six sound bananas; peel and halve them lengthwise. Spread them with jam, place in a deep pie-dish, and pour a pint of custard over (this may be made with custard powder). Put in a cold place to set.

190. BANANAS FRIED

Peel the bananas, slice them lengthwise, and fry them in lard. They can be served with sugar and a little lemon juice sprinkled on them.

191. BLACKBERRY CHARLOTTE RUSSE

Put slices of stale sponge to line the sides of a glass dish, and ripe blackberries in the centre. Pile whipped cream on top, and serve.

192. BLACKBERRY SPONGE

Fill an earthen bowl closely with small cubes of bread, pouring over the bread, as it is fitted into place, hot blackberry juice (blackberries cooked until soft, with sugar to taste, and passed through a sieve). Use all the juice the bread will absorb. Set the sponge aside in a cool place for some hours, then turn out of the bowl. Serve with blackberries, sugar, and cream.

193. CHERRY FLOAT

Strain the juice from one quart of stewed and sweetened cherries; thicken it with a teacupful of cornflour mixed smooth in cold water; add the juice of one lemon; let heat through and cool off; pour over the cherries in a glass dish.

194. CHESTNUT COMPOTE

Roast thirty chestnuts; take off the peel, and put them in a preserving-pan with a quarter of a pound of sugar and half a tumbler of cold water. Let them remain until the syrup is all absorbed. Take them out, arrange them in a glass dish, squeeze half a lemon over them, and sprinkle with fine sugar.

195. COOKED FRUIT SALAD

Have half a breakfastcupful each of apple-rings and of prunes, soaked overnight. Remove stones from prunes, add two breakfastcupfuls of seeded raisins, two tablespoonfuls of sugar, the juice of a lemon. Place these in a preserving-pan, let cook till tender; then add one breakfastcupful of stoned dates, and remove from fire. Let the salad grow cold. It should be served with cream or with an egg custard.

196. DATE CAKE

Take one pound of cheap dates, and two ounces of sweet almonds, blanched. Grease a small pudding-basin with cooking butter (basin a little larger than a breakfastcup). Arrange a cross at the bottom of it with split blanched almonds. Take out the stones of the dates, and in their place insert half-almonds;

then pack the dates in the basin (one at a time) as closely as possible—pressing them in tightly. When full, put a *heavy* weight on the dates—the size of the top of the basin—and let it stand twenty-four hours; then turn out of the basin (by slipping a thin knife round the sides of the basin) on to a plate—a green plate is best—and, when wanted, cut in thin slices (as you would a round cake). To be eaten for breakfast, tea, or supper, with a knife and fork and bread-and-butter.

197. DATES IN CUSTARD

Stone enough dates to cover the bottom of a glass dish, and put a blanched almond in each; pour over them one pint of custard, and serve cold.

198. DATE MOULD

Remove the stones from one pound of dates; chop up the fruit and put it into a lined pan, with the grated rind and the juice of a good-sized lemon. Just cover it with water, and set it to simmer. If the water simmers away, put a little more. Stir gently now and then, as it may stick and burn. When it becomes a thick paste, turn it into a wet mould, and when quite cold, turn it out and serve it with custard or whipped cream.

199. DATES STEWED

Wash one pound of dates, and leave them in a basin overnight, covered with one pint of cold water. Next morning, place in a pan with the same water, and when they come to the boil, let simmer gently for about ten minutes, or until tender, but not broken; add a few drops of lemon juice. Take out the dates, add a little sugar to the liquid, simmer until it thickens; then pour it over the fruit, and serve when cold.

200. FIGS, STEWED, No. I

Pulled figs are the best for this. They should be cooked very slowly, in as little water as possible, with a very little sugar, to taste, and a thin lemon rind, in the proportion of one lemon to the pound of figs. They

C 2—Puddings

should not swell out so as to assume a bloated appearance, which shows that they have *boiled* instead of stewing. Test with a silver fork when they are soft enough, and add about two teaspoonfuls of lemon juice before taking them out of the stewpan.

201. FIGS, STEWED, No. 2

Wash the figs thoroughly, cover with boiling water, and let cook until the skin is tender, adding more boiling water if needed. When about done, a little sugar may be added. Let the syrup cook until thickened a little. Serve hot or cold, with plain, whipped, or Devonshire cream. For a more elaborate dish, make an opening in the side of each fig and insert a teaspoonful of chopped nuts, or nuts and cherries; press into shape, and cook with care not to spoil shape.

202. FIGS, STEWED, No. 3

Steam the figs as in No. 203, then place them in boiling syrup and remove pan to side of stove for twenty minutes at least. Remove the fruit; boil down the syrup till it thickens, and pour it over the figs.

203. FIGS, STUFFED

Put some dried figs in a steamer (or enamelled colander, covered with a plate or lid) over boiling water. Steam till they expand and are soft. Scoop out the inside, and mix it with chopped nuts and a syrup of lemon juice and sugar. Roll in sugar, and serve.

204. FIGS, GREEN, BAKED

Place the figs in an earthenware dish which has a lid, adding a little lemon juice and sugar to taste: no water is necessary. Cover, and bake slowly until tender.

205. FIGS, GREEN, STEWED

Place the fruit in a lined pan, and let simmer till tender, which will be very soon, before adding sugar and flavouring; the latter may be ginger, lemon juice, rhubarb juice, or pineapple juice. Let a syrup form before the figs are removed, and pour off all together.

206. GOOSEBERRY FOOL

Take a quart of full-grown, unripe gooseberries; pick them, and put them into a saucepan with a cupful of water; cover them, and let them heat very slowly. When the gooseberries are soft, but not so much heated as to burst, strain the water from them. Bruise them to a fine pulp, or pass them through a sieve, with sufficient sugar to sweeten them. Let them stand till cool, and then mix milk or cream with them. Serve in a large bowl.

207. PEACH AND RICE MÉRINGUE

Arrange a border of boiled rice on a dish that will stand the heat of the oven. Surround this with halves of peaches, fresh or canned, with skins removed; inside the border place sliced peaches and rice in layers, sprinkling the peaches with sugar and giving the whole a dome shape. Cover with méringue, dust with sugar, and set in a slow oven for about ten minutes.

208. PEARS, BAKED AND STUFFED

Take large pears; peel, core, and stuff them with seeded raisins, stoned dates, chopped nuts, or shredded coconut, with some rather acid jam or marmalade. Place closely in a pan, with just enough water to prevent burning; bake slowly till tender. Remove into a warmed glass dish, and let cool. A plain cold custard may be poured over them before serving.

209. PEAR COMPOTE

Stew some pears whole in syrup (as No. 211); put them in a glass dish; have ready a pear fruit jelly, or a (packet) lemon jelly, and let cool. Boil the syrup until reduced and thick, then pour it over the jelly and pears. Serve cold.

210. PEARS AND RAISINS COMPOTE

Stem, peel, quarter, and core six medium, sound, sweet pears, then place in a small enamelled pan with a piece of cinnamon stick, six drops of vanilla essence, an ounce of granulated sugar, and enough water just to cover pears; let slowly boil for twenty-five minutes; add two ounces of seeded California raisins; shuffle pan and cook for ten minutes longer; remove cinnamon, pour fruit into a dish, and serve either hot or cold.

211. PEARS, STEWED

Take a quart of small cooking pears, and wipe but do not peel them. Place in a lined covered pan, with half a pint of sugar, some lemon peel in strips and a quarter of a pint of water. Cook slowly until tender. Serve hot or cold.

212. PRUNES, STEWED

Soak one pound of good prunes all night. Next day put them into a saucepan with the water in which they were soaked (about one pint), half a pound of loaf sugar, the thin rind of a lemon, and a stick of cinnamon. Simmer gently for four hours. Place the prunes in a glass dish, and strain the juice over them.

213. PRUNES, STUFFED

Prepare as for Stewed Prunes: in the morning remove the stones by making an incision at one end; fill the cavity with chopped or ground nuts, and sugar. Roll the prunes in powdered sugar, and let them dry.

214. RAISINS WITH RICE

Thoroughly wash and drain four ounces of Carolina rice, then place in enamelled saucepan with a pint of milk, three ounces of sugar, a vanilla stick, the rind of a quarter of a sound lemon, and a saltspoonful of salt. Lightly mix, and let gently boil for forty minutes; add three ounces of California seeded raisins; mix well and cook for fifteen minutes longer; remove vanilla and rind. Whisk up a gill of cream to a froth in bowl; add to rice and raisins; mix well; dress rice, etc., on a deep dish, and serve.

215. RHUBARB BAKED

Rinse quickly, wipe clean, and peel the larger stalks. Have ready an earthen dish with plate to fit the top as cover. Cut the stalks into this, in short lengths, scattering sugar over in layers; add one or two table-spoonfuls of water, cover, and set in the oven. In a short time the rhubarb will be tender, the syrup pink-coloured. A bit of ginger root or orange peel may be added while baking. Whole figs, dates, or raisins, previously boiled in hot water, may be put into the baking-dish with uncooked rhubarb, and cooked until the rhubarb is tender.

216. RHUBARB AND FIGS (OR DATES)

Have ready half a pound of figs which have been quartered and soaked in cold water overnight; or half a pound of dates, stoned, halved, and steeped. Add two tablespoonfuls of sugar to one pound of rhubarb (if dates are used, one tablespoonful of sugar), and mix the fruit in. Let it steam slowly along with the rhubarb until all is tender.

217. STRAWBERRY PYRAMID

Cook one pint of flaked rice; place a layer at the bottom of a deep glass dish, and spread one teaspoonful of butter over it. Next place a layer of strawberries, sprinkled with castor sugar; repeat until a pyramid is made. Serve with cream cold.

VARIOUS

218. COMBINATION FRUIT

Peel six ripe bananas, pulp them through a sieve, sweeten to taste; add one tablespoonful of orange juice and pile the mixture, in little heaps, each on a quarter-inch-thick round of pineapple. Place a large strawberry on top of each mound.

219. FRUIT AND NUT MACÉDOINE

Prepare lemon, orange, or wine jelly. Put a few spoonfuls in the bottom of a wetted mould. Arrange on this, when set, round slices of banana and split blanched almonds, in a symmetrical pattern. Cover with more jelly, let it set; put in a design of cut figs and dates, alternately with jelly and with more banana and almond, till the mould is full. Sweetened and flavoured whipped cream is an excellent adjunct to this, placed round the macédoine when turned out.

220. SOLID FRUIT BUTTER

Take equal parts of stoned raisins, dates, and figs. Weigh and add an equal weight to the whole in shelled and blanched nuts. The nuts may be of any sort or sorts, to taste, such as almonds, hazels, walnuts, Brazils, peanuts, cobs, etc. Mix all thoroughly, pack tightly into a mould or basin, and leave for two or three days with a heavy weight on top; then unmould, when the butter will be found solid and able to be thinly sliced. The fruit may be chopped, or passed through a mincer, and the nuts chopped or milled, if preferred.

CHAPTER VIII

PASTRY DISHES: FRUIT PIES, AMERICAN PIES, TARTS, AND OTHER PASTRIES

NOTE.—However many be the diatribes of doctors, the human heart clings closely to its pies. There is really no reason why properly prepared pastry should disagree with the average healthy person. It is not a mystery; it is pleasant alike to smell, touch, and taste; if it is the companion and the vehicle of wholesome fruits and sound preserves, its food-value is practically doubled. And it need not be expensive.

DEFINITIONS

Pastry consists of flour, into which "shortening," *i.e.*, fat, has been amalgamated by various methods, and which is then moistened by the addition of some liquid, usually cold water. It is divisible into several heads :

(1) *Plain, or "short" crust or pastry.*—In this, the shortening is mixed with the flour by rubbing with the finger-tips; or, if it be suet instead of butter, lard, dripping, etc., it is very finely chopped or grated and then mixed in.

(2) *Puff-paste or feuilletage.*—In this, the shortening is worked into a dough of flour and water, by means of folding and rolling, the result being a puffed-up texture of *leafage* (feuilletage), quite different from that of short crust.

(3) *Flaky pastry.*—In this, both the above methods are employed—*i.e.*, half the shortening is rubbed into the flour, which is then moistened, and the rest of the shortening is folded in, as for puff-paste.

(4) *Chopped paste.*—In this, the shortening is chopped into the flour in a chopping-bowl, until the mixture resembles meal; it is then moistened and rolled out once or twice.

(5) *American "biscuit" dough.*—Here the flour is

mixed with baking-powder, the shortening then rubbed in; it is then made into a soft slack paste with milk and water, and is rolled out and cut to the purpose required.

(The two following are not pastry in the strict sense, as one is made without shortening and one without flour.)

(6) *Potato paste.*—Mealy potatoes are boiled and mashed through a sieve. Flour is added to stiffen them, and cream to moisten them into a soft, easily workable paste.

(7) *Oatmeal paste.*—This consists simply of fine oatmeal mixed into a paste with boiling water.

MATERIALS

(1) *Flour.*—A fine " pastry " flour, which absorbs but little moisture, is the best. It should be sifted, and well dried by placing in the oven while the latter is getting warm.

(2) *Shortening.*—For puff-paste, butter is indispensable. For the rest, lard (which makes a soft, light-coloured crust), beef dripping (which gives especially " short " crisp results), clarified beef suet, alone or mixed with butter—and vegetable fats, such as margarine, may be employed. Mutton dripping by itself is inadvisable, having a hard, tallowy effect; but a good short crust for homely purposes can be made by using a mixture of mutton dripping, beef dripping, and bacon-fat, " run down " together a day or so before using.

(3) *Liquid.*—The water should be of the same temperature as that of the room where you make the pastry, which should *not* be the kitchen. Roughly speaking, use the coldest water you can get. Some chefs will have nothing but ice-water. *As little liquid as possible* is a safe rule. About half a breakfastcupful of water to two breakfastcupfuls of flour will be about the right proportion; but it depends upon the flour; some flour requires more liquid than others.

(4) Baking-powder (like " self-raising " flour) is the resort of the nervous or inexperienced pastry maker. It ensures lightness; but the expert does not need it.

I give several recipes which include baking-powder; but I repeat that it is not essential to good pastry.

(5) *Utensils.*—Have a good, smooth, heavy paste-board—but a marble slab is far the best if you can afford it; a rolling-pin, preferably with movable ends; a flour dredger; a chopping-bowl and knife; plenty of sizes in pie-dishes and of shapes in patty-pans; a good baking-tin or sheet.

(6) An oven kept at a given heat for a given time. Plenty of excellent pastry is spoilt by careless baking.

(Made paste can be kept uncooked for a day or two without injury, *provided it be covered to exclude all air, and kept in a cool place.* Cooked pastry will keep several days if in a dry place. It must be reheated carefully in a good hot oven : tepid, half-warm paste is unendurable.)

SOME GOLDEN RULES FOR PASTRY MAKING

1. Keep whatever utensils you use—pasteboard, roller, wooden spoons, dredger, in short, everything—perfectly clean and absolutely dry.
2. Use the coldest water you can get—iced water, for choice—to mix your paste with.
3. Sift your flour through a fine wire sieve; this lets the air through it, and removes any lumps.
4. If possible, use a marble slab instead of a board.
5. Make your pastry in the coolest place you can find. This especially applies to warm weather.
6. If you have hot or damp hands, touch your pastry as little as possible with them : use a knife instead.
7. Be sure to leave a ventilating hole in your pie-crust. The china chimneys sold for this purpose are excellent.
8. Do not let the oven door stand open to admit a cold draught upon pastry when it is being baked; and NEVER let pastry stand in a draught after being taken out.
9. In making fruit pies, fill the dish well, piling up the fruit towards the centre. Otherwise, when it shrinks during cooking, the paste will fall with it and into it, and become wet and soggy.
10. Clean up every utensil thoroughly before you put it away.

221. PUFF-PASTE, OR FEUILLETAGE

Sift one pound of flour on a small table; make a " bay " or " well " in the centre; pour into it half a pint of cold water, adding half a teaspoonful of salt. Briskly knead with the hand, gradually incorporating the flour until a perfect dough; then let rest for fifteen minutes.

Wash well a pound of good butter in a quart of cold water; then knead the butter on a table with the hand, give it a square flat form, and put in a cool place. Flour the table, roll out the paste to one-third larger than the butter, place the butter on top, fold up the four corners till they completely envelop the butter, then with the pastry roller roll out to one inch thick in a square form. Fold up the paste in three folds without separating. Roll it out from the top with the roller to one inch longer only, of a square form; this operation is usually termed " turn." Give the paste half a turn to the right with the hand, and roll it out to the same thickness as before; fold up the same as before—then the paste will have two " turns." Place it on a tin, enveloped in a towel, and let rest in a cool place for twenty minutes. Then give two more turns as before; let rest for twenty minutes again. Give two similar turns, and let rest in a cool place till required, always enveloped in a clean, slightly moistened towel.

Note.—It is best to protect puff-paste in the oven by a piece of paper until it has attained its full height. If originally made a quarter of an inch thick, it should rise about two inches. It may be necessary to shift its position in the oven, so that it may rise evenly all round.

222. RICH SHORT CRUST FOR FRUIT PIES

Rub seven ounces of butter into eight ounces of flour; add one teaspoonful of castor sugar, the yolk of one egg, one teaspoonful of baking-powder, a pinch of salt, and just enough cold water (about one-eighth of a pint should suffice) to mix a very stiff paste, which should be rolled out once only.

223. " CHOPPED " PASTE

Place in a chopping-bowl three breakfastcupfuls of flour with half a teaspoonful each of salt and of baking-powder, well sifted and mixed. Take two-thirds of a breakfastcupful of shortening and chop it into the flour, keeping the knife well floured. When every particle of fat is coated with flour, so that the mixture looks like meal, gradually add sufficient cold water to make it into a paste; which should not be crumbly or sticky, but should come away cleanly from the knife and the sides of the bowl. (It should be mixed with another knife than the chopper.) Roll it with the knife into a ball, and when the sides of the bowl are quite free of any dough on them, put it on a floured paste-board and pat it out into a square with the rolling-pin. Do not touch it with your fingers more than you can help, and use no more dredging flour than is absolutely necessary, but the paste must not stick either to the board or roller. The paste can be used at once, or it can be set aside, *closely covered,* for some hours, when it will be found more easily workable.

224. FLAKY PASTRY

Take half a breakfastcupful of butter; wash it well in cold water until smooth and pliable; pat it into a smooth flat cake, and set it aside in a cool place. Have three breakfastcupfuls of flour mixed with half a teaspoonful of salt; rub into the flour half a cupful of shortening (lard, dripping, etc.) until the mixture looks like meal. Mix it to a paste (using a knife) with not more than three-quarters of a cupful of cold water—less if possible. Knead it slightly, cover it up, and let stand for five minutes. Pat it with the rolling-pin, and roll out into a square or oblong sheet; then fold in the butter as for puff-paste, giving the paste two or three " turns," and letting it stand for five minutes between each turn. This may be used at once or set aside *closely covered.*

225. PASTE FOR ONE LARGE AMERICAN OR PLATE PIE

Sift half a pound of flour on a table. Make a " fountain " (hollow space) in the centre; place into it one ounce and a half of butter, one gill of cold water, and one saltspoonful and a half of salt; then with the hand mix the butter, water, and salt briskly for three minutes, and gradually and slowly incorporate the flour with the rest, mixing for five minutes. Lay the paste on a plate, cover it with a towel, and place in a cool place to rest for a few minutes. Have ready three ounces of well-washed butter in a lump; return the paste to the table, flatten it lightly, then place the lump of butter in the centre; fold over the edges so as to enclose the butter, roll it out lengthwise with the pastry-roller, and refold the paste into three folds. Let it rest again in a cool place for three minutes; then roll it again, fold it as before, and set in an ice-box, if possible, for five minutes.

To make the pie.—Cut out half the prepared paste, and roll it out round, ten inches in diameter. Lightly butter a pie-plate nine and a half inches in diameter. Arrange the paste nicely over it. Take the mincemeat, cooked or uncooked fruit, or whatever the pie is to be filled with—one pound and a half will be required for this size pie; lay it over the lined pie-plate; evenly flatten it, leaving one inch clear around the edge of the plate; take the remaining half of the paste, roll it out round, fold it in two, and with a knife make three light incisions each half an inch in the centre. Lightly moisten the edge of the plate with beaten egg, then cover with the paste, pressing it down with the hands all around the edge so as to entirely enclose the preparation, and then moisten the surface with beaten egg. Place it in a moderate oven to bake for forty minutes. Remove it to the oven door, liberally sprinkle powdered sugar over; return it to the oven, close the door for two minutes so as to have the sugar entirely melted. Remove from the oven, and serve either hot or cold.

226. PLAIN " BISCUIT " DOUGH

Take one quart of flour; mix with two rounded tea-spoonfuls of baking-powder and one teaspoonful of salt; rub in a heaped tablespoonful of shortening—such as butter, lard, dripping, etc. Make a " bay " in the centre, pour in one pint of new milk, or milk and water mixed, and mix a soft dough, bringing in the flour from the sides, lightly, and with as little mixing as possible. Roll out, cut out for purpose required, and bake quickly.

" This is a useful dough for dumplings. The term " biscuit " is used in the American sense, which means a crisp bread.

PASTRY MADE WITHOUT SHORTENING

227. POTATO PASTE

Boil enough mealy potatoes to make, when mashed up, three-quarters of a pint, or three-quarters of a pound; add enough flour to stiffen the potatoes well, and half a teaspoonful of salt. Moisten with cream until soft enough to roll out easily. Bake in quick oven.

228. OATMEAL PASTE

To two cupfuls of fine oatmeal add one cup of boiling water. Mix thoroughly, roll out thin. If used for open tarts or American pies, bake lightly before putting in the contents.

FRUIT PIES

Note.—These are *covered over* with crust, which rests upon a rim of paste : the pie-crust of the proverb, " made to be broken." And they are made in pie-dishes (sometimes known as pudding-dishes), not in any way to be confused with pie-plates.

The standard pie is Apple Pie; all other fruit pies conform more or less to that historic model. " Cherry pie is very nice," as Jenny Wren said; and according to Southey's poem, " Gooseberry pie is best." Black currant pie is by many folks considered a feast for the gods; but there is no fruit so cheap or so humble that it may not be used, *solus*, or in combination with some other fruit, for the concocting of a pie.

Some people always cook, or half-cook, the fruit, before pie-ing it. This saves the subsequent shrinkage of the fruit, and possible decline and fall of the pastry owing to that shrinkage; but it dissipates some of the fruit's flavour. However, recipes are given for both this method and that employed with raw fruit. Stone fruits should be washed and wiped before using.

Fruit pies for ordinary use are usually made with " short " or with " flaky " crust. They may be glazed with whisked white of eggs, and a little sugar subsequently sifted over; or by lightly brushing the top with cold water and then dusting it liberally with castor sugar; or by brushing with one teaspoonful of sugar dissolved in two teaspoonfuls of milk. When not glazed, the pie should be dusted with castor sugar.

Ventilation is best effected by the china " chimney " sold for the purpose; its shoulders sustain the paste as an inverted egg-cup can never do. Moreover, the slit made over the inverted egg-cup, as a rule, only ventilates the egg-cup itself.

A good oven is essential. Test it by putting in a little flour, which will blacken if the oven be too hot. If it becomes pale brown, the oven is right for your pie. Set it in the hottest part of the oven for the first five to ten minutes, and then shift it to a somewhat cooler part.

229. APPLE PIE

(About half a pound of short, of flaky, or of puff paste, should suffice for any of the following.)

Take two pounds of cooking apples; peel, core, and slice them rather thickly. Roll out your paste into an oval shape, about half an inch thick : it should be larger than you require to cover the pie with. Line the rim with paste, put in half the fruit, then add two table-spoonfuls of moist sugar, and flavouring—either a little grated nutmeg, four or five cloves, or cinnamon, or a saltspoonful of grated lemon rind. Grated ginger is liked by some people. *No* water should be added. Put in the rest of the apples, brush the rim paste with water, put the cover on, press the rim and cover edges together, and notch them with a sharp knife or clean scissors. Place in a hot oven for forty to fifty minutes.

Many consider an apple pie incomplete without a few slices of quince; and some add half a wineglassful of sherry.

230. SCOTCH APPLE PIE

Peel and core some apples; place them (whole) in an earthenware dish in a slow oven until quite tender; then place in a pie-dish, with four ounces of picked sultana raisins to every pound of fruit. Sprinkle with sugar and grated lemon, cover with pastry, and bake quickly. This can be eaten either hot or cold.

231. BLACKBERRY PIE

One pound and a half of blackberries, well picked; or, better, one pound of blackberries and half a pound of apples, peeled, cored, and sliced; four ounces of sugar. Time to bake, thirty-five to forty-five minutes.

232. BLACK CURRANT PIE

One pound and a half of black currants, well stemmed; four ounces of sugar. Time to bake, about forty minutes.

233. CHERRY PIE

Take one pound and a half of stemmed cherries and two tablespoonfuls of sugar. Proceed as for Apple Pie, No. 1. About forty minutes to cook.

234. CURRANT AND RASPBERRY PIE

Use one pint and a half of picked currants, half a pint of raspberries, three large tablespoonfuls of sugar. Proceed as for Apple Pie, No. 1. This will take about forty-five minutes to bake.

235. DAMSON PIE

Use one pound and a half of damsons and proceed as for Apple Pie No. 1. This will take about twenty minutes longer than the apple pie to cook.

236. FLAN ANGLAISE

Have half a pound of pie paste (see p. 83) rolled out on a floured paste-board; lightly butter a deep plate, and line it with the paste, well pressing the paste down along the rim, and trimming it off neatly. At the bottom of the plate spread four tablespoonfuls of apple jelly; over this, put six good apples, peeled, cored, and thinly sliced; arrange them nicely so as to lie flat. Sprinkle them with a mixture of two ounces of castor sugar and one teaspoonful of powdered cinnamon. Bake for half an hour; when the flan is done, spread two tablespoonfuls of red currant jelly over the top, and serve hot.

237. GOOSEBERRY PIE, No. I

Have gooseberries stewed till tender in a very little water; add sugar to taste. Crush fruit a little; add one dessertspoonful each of flour and butter; mix well in. Place in pie-dish with pastry-lined rim, and cover with short crust. Bake in good oven.

238. GOOSEBERRY PIE, No. 2

Top and tail one pint and a half of gooseberries, and proceed as for Apple Pie, using four ounces of sugar. Forty minutes to bake.

239. MULBERRY PIE

Take one pint of ripe mulberries, remove the stalks, put the fruit into an aluminium pan, add two ounces of sugar and the juice of one lemon. Let simmer slowly for thirty minutes, or until the mulberries are soft; then put them into a pie-dish, which must be lined half-way down with " short " pie-crust. Cover like any other fruit pie, trim and scallop the edges, and bake in a moderate oven.

240. PLUM PIE

Proceed as for Cherry Pie. Thirty to forty minutes to bake.

241. RAISIN PIE

Take two breakfastcupfuls of seeded raisins, soak them overnight in water, just enough to cover them; next day, add half a breakfastcupful of sugar, and put them in a pan to simmer until quite tender. Strain off most of the water, add the juice of one lemon, thicken with one tablespoonful of flour (mixed smooth in a very little cold water) and cook again for a quarter of an hour. Have a flat plate lined with paste, spread the mixture over it, put a pastry cover on top, and bake lightly; or substitute for the pastry cover a méringue top. For children, who like things " crunchy," some shelled, blanched, and chopped nuts of any kind can be mixed with the raisins. This provides a wholesome and nourishing dish.

242. RAISIN AND MINT TURNOVERS

Chop finely half a pound of seeded raisins, and enough fresh green mint to fill about a breakfastcup when chopped. Add one teaspoonful each of granulated sugar and of fresh butter; mix the ingredients thoroughly. Spread the mixture on squares of short pastry, moisten edges, double the squares over, either oblong or triangular, and bake in moderate oven.

243. RHUBARB PIE

This is often made with puff-paste, and it is advisable to pile the rhubarb extra high, as it shrinks in cooking more than fruit, especially stone fruit. Cut the rhubarb (having peeled it, unless it is forced, or very young) into inch lengths. It may be used alone, or mixed with an equal quantity of gooseberries. Sweeten well with four ounces of sugar at least. Bake about thirty-five to forty minutes.

244. WHORTLEBERRY (OR BILBERRY) PIE

Line the rim of a baking-dish with short crust and fill centre with the berries; add half a tablespoonful of butter, two tablespoonfuls of sugar, and one table-spoonful each of flour and water. Squeeze a little lemon juice in; cover with crust, and bake in good oven.

AMERICAN PIES

Note.—These immensely popular Transatlantic dishes are like our English pies only in one respect, the funda-mental fact of being covered. Otherwise, instead of being deep, they are shallow; instead of being oval, they are round; instead of occupying pie-dishes, they are made in plates.

The pastry may be either " short," " chopped," or " flaky "—puff-paste is rarely, if ever, used. For a very soft filling, such as custard or pumpkin, some cooks prefer a suet paste.

The general formula runs as follows : Take a per-forated tin pie-plate (if you can get one), or an ordinary pudding plate; roll out your paste, one-eighth of an inch thick, into a round piece a little larger than the plate; place the paste in the plate, so as to fit well and exclude any air from beneath. Do not stretch the paste : it must cover the plate loosely. Brush it with lightly whisked white of egg; this forms a film over the paste and prevents it getting wetted by the juice of the filling.

Put in the filling; moisten the rim of the paste by brushing lightly with cold water; cut a second round of paste rather larger than the first, for cover; put it on, and trim neatly.   A rim of paste, three-quarters of an inch wide, may be inserted, if desired, between the under and upper crusts.   Cut several ventilation slits in the top crust, *before* you put it on, and place the pie in a slow oven. It should take thirty-five to forty-five minutes to bake, but must brown well.   If you wish to glaze it, beat one yolk, add one tablespoonful of water and half a tablespoonful of sugar, beat again, and lightly brush the upper crust with the mixture.   This may be done either just before the pie goes into the oven or just before it is ready to come out.

245. APPLE PIE

Peel, core, and slice six apples; place in a bowl with two ounces of sugar and one teaspoonful of vanilla essence; turn them well in the seasoning, then proceed to prepare and bake the pie.

246. APPLE PIE, " MOTHER'S "

Fill the space between the crusts with apples, sliced thin, rounding up the slices so as to make a very full pie; add two or three tablespoonfuls of water and bake in a slow oven.   When done, with a sharp knife cut around the pie between the two crusts and carefully lift up the upper crust.   To the apples add half a cupful or more of sugar, a few grains of salt, a tablespoonful of butter, and a grating of nutmeg; mix thoroughly with a silver spoon or knife, spread evenly over the crust; replace the upper crust, pressing it down to meet the apple, if necessary, and sift powdered sugar over the top.   Serve, when slightly cooled, with cream and sugar.

247. BERRY PIES (CURRANTS, RASPBERRIES, ETC.)

To a scant pint of berries add two tablespoonfuls of flour, half a cupful or more of sugar, and a scant half teaspoonful of salt; mix and put into the plate lined with pastry; add bits of butter here and there, finish with a second crust, and bake in a very slow oven.

Brush the paste with white of egg before putting in the berries. Brush the edge of the under crust with water, before the edge of the upper crust is pressed upon it; press or pinch the two edges together. But even with this precaution the juice is liable to leak out.

248. GREENGAGE PIE

Roll out on a lightly floured table one pound of pie-paste in two separate equal parts about a quarter of an inch thick. Lightly butter a pie-plate, then line the plate with one of the parts of paste; press it well all round the edges, and trim. Remove the stones from a quart of greengages, place them in a bowl; season with one ounce of sugar and one teaspoonful of vanilla essence; mix well, then arrange them in the pie-plate; lightly egg the edges all round, arrange the other layer of paste over, and press both edges together all round. Make a few incisions on the surface, and with a hair pastry-brush lightly glaze the top with beaten egg. Set to bake in the oven for thirty minutes; remove, dredge a little powdered sugar over, and serve either hot or cold.

249. PEACH PIE

Open a pint can of fine peaches; slice into thin slices; sprinkle three tablespoonfuls of fine sugar over them; thoroughly mix. Prepare a pie-paste, and proceed to finish the pie the same way.

250. PEAR PIE, No. I

Remove the stems and peel eight medium, good, sound, fresh pears; cut them in halves, remove the seeds, then cut into slices and place in a bowl. Season with two ounces of vanilla sugar and half a teaspoonful of ground cinnamon; turn them well in the seasoning; then proceed to make the pie.

251. PEAR PIE, No. 2

Peel and cut in half eight medium, sound pears; remove the seeds, then finely slice them and place in a bowl. Season with one ounce of sugar and one teaspoonful of ground cinnamon. Mix well. Line a lightly buttered pie-plate with a thin pie-paste. Place the pears in the pie-plate, lightly egg the edges of the plate; cover the pears with another similar layer of pie-paste; make a few small incisions on the surface, and press down the two layers of paste around the border of the plate; lightly egg the surface. Set to bake in the oven for thirty minutes. Remove, let rest on a table for five minutes, sprinkle a little powdered sugar over, and serve either hot or cold.

252. PLUM PIE

Remove the stems from a pint of canned or fresh plums; place them on a plate, and dredge two table-spoonfuls of powdered sugar over them; mix well, then proceed to make the pie.

253. PRUNE PIE

Soak one pound of dry prunes in plenty of cold water for ten hours; remove stones, drain well, wipe thoroughly, and place in a bowl with four ounces of sugar and half a teaspoonful of ground cinnamon; mix well for a minute, and then proceed to finish the pie.

254. RHUBARB PIE

Carefully scrape the skin of one pound of sound, fresh rhubarb, cut into one-inch pieces, then place in a saucepan with four ounces of granulated sugar and one teaspoonful of cornstarch. Set the pan on a brisk fire, stir well with a wooden spoon, and let briskly cook for fifteen minutes, frequently stirring meanwhile. Prepare a pie-paste, and proceed to finish the pie.

TARTS

Note.—These are open shells of pastry, containing fruit, jam, custard, etc., and having no cover; their nearest approach to a cover being a twisted lattice-work of pastry which is now rarely seen.

These tarts may be made with either puff, short, or flaky crust; the rich short crust (No. 222) is also appropriate, or that indicated in the formula for American pie-paste (p. 83).

255. APPLE TART

Stew some tart cooking apples, pared and cored but not sliced, in as little water as possible. When they are tender (but not broken), place them in a pie-dish, and put a little orange marmalade into the cavity of each. Line the edges of the dish with thin paste, make a lattice work of pastry-strips across the top, and bake light-brown in a quick oven.

256. DATE TART, No. I

Remove the stones from the dates; stew in a small quantity of water until soft enough to strain through a colander. To one cupful and a half of date pulp add one egg, beaten slightly, a scant half-teaspoonful each of salt and cinnamon, and one cupful and a half of milk. Bake with an under crust only.

257. DATE TART, No. 2

Take one pound of dates; wash, and put with one quart of milk in a lined pan to simmer until tender enough to stone and pass through a sieve or colander. Thicken with a beaten egg, or with a teaspoonful of cornflour mixed smooth in milk. Have ready a baked shell of pastry; place the fruit in this, and put a little whipped cream on top.

258. AMERICAN LEMON TART

Line a French fireproof china pie-dish with a short crust. Grate the rind of a lemon, and squeeze the juice. Put a tablespoonful of cornflour into a basin, moisten it with cold water, pour a cupful of boiling water on it, and stir it till slightly thickened; add the rind and juice of the lemon, one ounce of butter, two ounces of sugar, and one beaten egg. Pour this mixture into the pie-dish, and bake in a moderate oven. Serve cold with sifted sugar over.

259. GREENGAGE TARTLETS

Carefully split fifteen tinned greengages and remove the stones. Have three ounces of powdered sugar and one gill of cold water in a saucepan, and boil for five minutes; then add the greengages, and cook for ten minutes. Place them in a bowl, and proceed to finish the tartlets.

260. RHUBARB TARTLETS

Neatly trim one pound of fresh rhubarb, remove the fibres, wash in cold water, drain and cut in pieces one inch long. Place in a small saucepan with four ounces of fine sugar and half a teaspoonful of vanilla essence. Mix well with a wooden spoon, cover the pan, set on the fire, and let gently cook for twenty minutes, being careful to frequently stir at the bottom meantime.

Prepare six tartlet crusts, and fill with the rhubarb preparation. Dredge a little fine sugar over, and serve.

VARIOUS PASTRY

261. APPLE DUMPLINGS, BAKED, No. I

Prepare a pie-paste. Roll it on a lightly floured table to the thickness of one-fifth of an inch. Cut out six pieces, each three inches square.

Peel and core six small apples; lay each apple right side up on top of each piece of paste in the centre. Fill the hollow from which the core has been scooped with granulated sugar, mixed with half a teaspoonful of ground cinnamon, then fold up the corners of the paste on top of each apple so as to entirely close them. Cut from the remaining paste six round pieces about one inch in diameter; arrange each piece on top of each apple. With a small pastry brush gently moisten the tops, edges, and sides with a beaten egg. Lay them on a baking-pan, and set in a moderate oven to bake for thirty-five minutes. Remove, dress on a dish, and serve with a hard sauce separately.

262. APPLE DUMPLINGS, BAKED, No. 2

Pare and core some good-sized cooking apples; fill the centres with sugar. Cut your paste, which should be rolled rather thin in squares large enough to cover apples. Place an apple in the centre of each square, bring the corners together on top, and pinch them securely together. Lay them closely in a baking-pan, and pour in a syrup made with one pint of water and one pound of sugar; this should cover the dumplings half-way up. Sprinkle them with cinnamon, and bake in a brisk oven from forty to forty-five minutes.

263. APPLE DUMPLNGS, No. 3

Proceed as above, but with the syrup omitted. A good short crust is essential.

264. APPLE JONATHAN

Take some bread dough and work butter into it till it is quite " short." Line the sides of a pie-dish with it; fill the centre with peeled, sliced, and cored apples, into which should be mixed sugar, butter, and spice to taste. Put a thick pastry cover on, and bake well; then unmould upon a hot dish, with the cover upside down. Some persons add the sugar, etc., at this point. Serve hot.

265. APPLE SLUMP

Make a biscuit dough (as per No. 226) with one pint and a half of flour; mix in two beaten eggs and two quarts of peeled, cored, and chopped apples, with sugar to taste. Put the mixture half an inch thick, into a buttered baking-pan, and bake it in a quick oven.

266. APPLE TURNOVERS

Roll out some short pastry rather thin; divide into squares; place stewed apple in the middle of each square, and fold the corners over so as to make a three-cornered turnover. Pinch together securely, prick with a fork, and bake in quick oven.

267. MINCE PIES

Line some patty-pans with good puff paste, rolled out about a quarter of an inch thick; fill with mince-meat, and cover with paste a trifle thicker. Cut the edges neatly; place in a brisk oven for twenty-five minutes. Remove, glaze with white of egg whisked stiff, dust with castor sugar, and replace in oven for a minute or so, to set the glaze. Serve hot.

268. SULTANA PUFFS

Excellent and wholesome puffs can be made, to use up any short crust left over from a pie, by rolling out the paste a quarter of an inch thick, cutting it in rounds, and placing about one tablespoonful of picked sultanas in the centre of each. Moisten the edges and turn over in three flaps, to make a three-cornered puff. Bake in moderate oven.

269. TREACLE GEORGE

Take a shallow cake-tin, or a deep plate, or a pie-dish; butter it. Place at the bottom a layer of pastry (short-crust) about a quarter of an inch thick; over this put a layer of treacle; over this a layer of fine bread-crumbs, sufficient to hide the treacle; over this squeeze a little lemon juice; then put a layer of pastry, and go on in the same rotation till the tin is filled up to the height of three or four inches or so. Bake in a fairly quick oven, remove from tin, and serve either hot or cold. This is a wholesome and attractive dish for children.

270. TREACLE PIE

Line a deep pie-dish with an undercrust; mix half a pint of treacle with a tablespoonful of flour; add the juice of a lemon and the rind and juicy pulp chopped fine (do not use any of the white pith). Moisten the edges, and cover with a crust; bake, and eat while hot.

Lightning Source UK Ltd.
Milton Keynes UK
UKOW050132221111

182436UK00004B/18/P